The WetSand WaveCast® Guide

to

Surf Forecasting

The WetSand WaveCast® Guide

to

Surf Forecasting

A simple approach to planning the perfect sessions.

Nathan Todd Cool

iUniverse, Inc.
New York Lincoln Shanghai

The WetSand WaveCast® Guide to Surf Forecasting
A simple approach to planning the perfect sessions.

iUniverse, Inc.

For information address:
iUniverse, Inc.
2021 Pine Lake Road, Suite 100
Lincoln, NE 68512
www.iuniverse.com

ISBN: 0-595-30365-X

Printed in the United States of America

This book is dedicated to you. Thank you for helping to make WetSand WaveCast®
the popular, free forecasting service that it is today.

Contents

List of Illustrations

Introduction

In my first book, *The Four Keys to Successful Design*, I wrote a chapter about the surf forecasting service I founded in the mid-1990s, WaveCast®, and its successful merger with WetSand.com. That chapter, "Necessity is a Mother", explained how my love for surfing and desire to plan my sessions well in advance gave birth to the free forecasting service we provide on the Internet today. I found that I wasn't alone on my quest for accurate surf forecasts, and that others had the same need I did.

At WetSand WaveCast® we attempt to fill that need with free surf forecast reports, swell graphs, wind charts, and e-mail notices. But this fills only a partial need for water sport enthusiasts like you. This book sets out to help fill the remaining void, giving you the upper hand on the essentials of surf forecasting.

Since the early, dawning days of WaveCast®, we've put in a lot of hard work watching countless swells, predicting their arrival, size, and conditions, and providing the services that break this all down. Now I'd like to share some of our experience with you, showing how you too can create surf forecasts and plan your sessions well in advance.

To plan the "perfect" session, every surfer, windsurfer, and body boarder needs to be familiar with the ever-changing state of the ocean. Surfing, for instance, requires knowledge extending beyond the basics of paddling out, popping up, hanging ten, pulling off a floater, snapping off the lip, and pulling out with grace. It also requires wisdom of what to expect from the ocean at any given time, especially if you want to plan a day off from work or school and not be skunked with ankle slapping boat wakes, or overpowered by thunderous mountains of water tossing harbor ships onto land.

When I've talked to people who haven't surfed—but want to—I usually hear the same thing: "I've skied all my life. Surfing should be no problem for me." Or I might hear, "I water ski, so surfing should be a breeze." I always get a kick out of those responses, knowing the surprise most newcomers get during their initiation to ocean water sports like surfing. I can empathize, because I was there once myself—shocked many a time by the power of the ocean, and the relentless beating it can dole out.

What many of us don't realize during our novice days of sea-sport activities is that the ocean is a different playing field, and we don't have the home-court advantage. Skiing has a predictable hill and slope that stays somewhat constant. Water-skiing has some varying conditions, but it's still fairly much a sport of constant value when it comes to the Mother Nature factor. Wave riding sports however, have many more variables to deal with.

Surfing, windsurfing, body boarding, and other such water sports are at the mercy of one of Earth's most formidable forces: the power of the ocean. This vast expanse, covering more than 70% of our planet with water, is a force to be reckoned with. The sea truly has life—not just in its fish, mammals, plankton, coral, and various creatures—but also in the energy that creates our waves, swings our tides, and influences our weather.

Besides just knowing when swells will arrive, and how big waves will be, we also need to account for wind, tidal depths, hazards, water temperatures, and other fluctuations that Mother Nature is known to vary at her whim. All of these factors have a science unto themselves. Knowing some of that science may not only satisfy your curiosity, but also help you get the most from your time in the water.

My hope is that this book will give you knowledge and insight into the sciences behind surf forecasting so you can further refine our forecasts, and using free, publicly available data plan your time with precision by knowing the when, where, how and why of surf forecasting. It's like that old Chinese proverb:

> *Give a man a fish and you feed him for a day. Teach a man to fish and you feed him for a lifetime.*

Although we thoroughly enjoy making the WaveCast® surf reports, and we plan to continue providing our free services at wetsand.com, we'd like to pass along the essentials that make this happen, empowering you to plan the *perfect* sessions.

In addition to the free surf forecasts provided by our WaveCast® service at wetsand.com, we also provide links to data to help you get involved with the forecast predictions. This data is there to help you take our forecasts one-step further, to refine the predictions for your region so you can judge the best of conditions and worst of conditions for your favorite breaks. Some of this information may be foreign to you. Nevertheless, with some practical knowledge of the forecasting basics, you can turn this information to your advantage, maximizing your time in (and out) of the water.

Surf forecasting is a science. As an engineer, I don't have a degree in meteorology, and I'm by no means an oceanographer. Nevertheless, over time I've used scientific approaches to surf forecasting, some of which are simplified variations of ocean physics and wave dynamics. Although there are intricacies to wave prediction, I can tell you that it doesn't take a rocket scientist to predict when swells will arrive, and how big their waves will be. This stuff isn't brain surgery—it may be simpler then you think. If you can use a basic calculator, this book will guide you through simple steps that you can use to forecast surfing conditions within a fair amount of accuracy.

This book is not intended as a guide to oceanography or sciences of surface wave analysis. Instead, this book illustrates simplified approaches to quickly and efficiently estimate surf forecast predictions based on higher-level scientific studies, and our first hand observations over the years. This book will show how you can quickly and easily predict swell arrival times, wave size, water temps, tides, winds and more using free, publicly available data. Combining this with our free WaveCast® forecasting services at wetsand.com, you'll get the most out of your sessions by knowing more about each swell headed your way, how the winds will behave, when the tides will cooperate, and other elements associated with a *perfect* session.

Throughout this book, I've included maps, models, and other tools for reference. There are 43 diagrams in all. However, to keep this book reasonably priced, a couple cutbacks were necessary.

- First, we had to convert the images to black and white. Leaving them as color would have increased the price of this book dramatically.

- Second, many of the maps, models, and figures showing other data are from public domain web sites like NOAA, NCEP, CDIP, etc. The original images are low resolution, making them a challenge to work with. The content on them however is clearly legible, and they do a great job at getting their points across. But still, they are low resolution, and don't necessarily get high marks in prettiness.

The last thing any of us wanted was to price this book too high. We wanted the information in this book to be well within your reach. I apologize for the not-so-perfect quality of the 43 images in this book, but I hope you'll agree that they are worth the cost-savings passed on to you.

Some subjects in this book may already be familiar to you. Nevertheless, this book will attempt to cover all the bases for surf forecasting; some you may want to skip over that you're familiar with, and others you may want to delve into deeper. In this book, we'll be covering the following topics:

- **Wave Anatomy**: Here we'll clarify the components that comprise a wave, and define some terms used throughout this book.

- **Understanding Models**: In this chapter, we'll take a quick look at how to read models, understanding their format and nomenclature, and how they represent our spherical world in a "flat" manner.

- **Basic Geography**: Quite often, we'll reference various points around the globe, which we'll point out in this chapter. We'll also briefly explain the coordinate system.

- **The Origin of Waves**: In this chapter we'll answer such questions as, "How are waves made?" and, "Where do they come from?"

- **Winds**: We'll explain this vital element to forecasting in simple terms. We'll also show how you can use free, publicly available data to forecast winds, and see how this affects surfing conditions as well.

- **Knowing When**: This chapter will show a simple method to estimate swell arrival time. We'll be doing a little math in this chapter, but don't let that scare you off; it's easier than you may think. We'll work through three examples forecasting swell arrival for various regions.

- **Knowing How Big**: As this chapter's name implies, this section will discuss how to forecast wave size for the swells you're tracking.

- **Mitigating Factors**: Not all is as it seems. There are many variables to consider when preparing an accurate forecast, and this chapter will explain these factors in depth.

- **Tides**: What makes the tides? How do these affect your surf? We'll dig deep into this subject so you can utilize this force of nature to your advantage.

- **Tropical Cyclones**: These rogue monsters not only wreak havoc, but can also give some decent surf, if they follow the right path. We'll take a look at the "how" and "why", and then work through an example, forecasting surf from a massive hurricane from September 2002: Hernan.

- **Seasonal Effects**: Timing is everything, and so are our seasons. But there are other factors to consider when looking at the season ahead. We'll take a closer look at these events.

- **Logging**: After seeing what it takes to forecast surf conditions, I'll illustrate some example logs you can use to keep track of the swell headed your way.

- **Now Casts**: Great! You forecasted when a swell would hit. But did it really happen? How can you tell without actually driving down to the beach?

- **Hazards**: Surf forecasting is more than looking out for fun waves to surf. It's also knowing what to avoid, recognizing beforehand the conditions to stay clear of.

- **Water Temperature**: Ever wonder why you might hit a summer session warm enough to trunk it, just to freeze your knees off the next day with a massive dip in water temps? We'll look at this, and ways to forecast it as well.

After all that, and passing along some parting thoughts, this book will provide you with free resources on the Internet to access data discussed in this book, as well as a glossary, and appendices for conversion data.

The one subject that we won't be covering in this book, and is important to predicting the *perfect* session, is the weather. This topic alone could fill another book. Nevertheless, there are plenty of free resources to access weather information through newspapers, television, radio, and the Internet. I've included some of the Internet resources for weather in the "Resources" chapter near the end of this book.

We have a lot to cover, but we'll take it one step at a time.

So let's get down to it—forecasting surf conditions, and planning the *perfect* sessions.

1

Wave Anatomy

o o o o o o o o o o o o o o o o o o o o o o o o o o o o o o o o o

The sea heaves up, hangs loaded o'er the land,
Breaks there, and buries its tumultuous strength.

—*Robert Browning*

We ride them, we duck dive under them, and at times, we get pummeled by them. All of us know what waves are. But there is a science behind these waves, which we'll be exploring throughout this book to understand how we can predict them.

Each chapter in this book is a step towards knowing more and more of the science of surf forecasting. Our first step along this journey is to make sure we're on the same page starting out. So I'd like to take a moment and quickly cover the basic terms that will help to set the stage for the next few chapters, and beyond.

In this chapter, we'll take a brief look at the components that comprise a wave. The Glossary near the end of this book contains the terms illustrated in this chapter, as well as other important terminology used throughout this book. The terms used here however, are the basic fundamentals, illustrated in Figure 1.

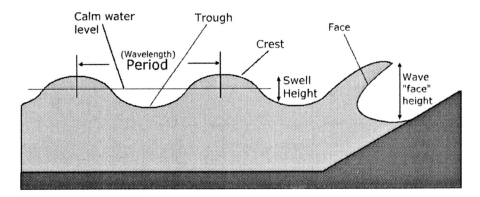

Figure 1 Anatomy of a Wave

Face: The Face is the front of a breaking wave. This has unique properties that differ from other heights and portions of waves out at sea.

Crest: The crest refers to the top of a wave. This term refers to waves forming far out to sea, as well as breaking waves near the shore. In both cases, it always refers to the top of the wave.

Trough: The trough is the bottom of a wave. Note that a trough is somewhat constant for waves until they near the shore. Breaking waves have a deeper trough.

Period: The period is the time between the crest of one wave to the crest of the next wave.

Wavelength: The wavelength is the distance between the crest of one wave to the crest of the next wave.

Swell Height: Often referred to as wave height, the swell height is the open ocean wave height, which is different from the actual face height of a breaking wave.

Wave Face Height: The face height is the size of the front (face) of the wave, measured from the trough in front of the wave to the top of the crest. This is higher than the swell height since the trough tends to be lower on a breaking wave. The reason for the increase in size on the face of the wave has a lot to do with shoaling and refraction, which we'll discuss in Chapter 7, "Knowing How Big", and in Chapter 8, "Mitigating Factors".

There's been a lot of controversy concerning the size, and face height of breaking waves. Some surfers like to report on the swell height, and some on the face height. Other methods, including the "Hawaiian" method use various formulas to judge big waves. In the WaveCast® surf reports, we prefer to use the face height, since this is what those surfing the waves will see. This height is usually bigger than the swell height, as illustrated in Figure 1.

Now that we have the basics, let's take a look at the most common forecasting tools we'll be using: models.

2

Understanding Models

"The seas are the heart's blood of the earth."

—*Henry Beston*

One summer day back in 1997, I was sitting on the beach in Malibu, California watching a longboard surfing competition that I had partly sponsored to promote the WaveCast® service. The big news that year was the massive El Niño predicted for the upcoming winter. The media was all over that story, even during those summer months, long before the effects of El Niño would hit the California region. It was hard to imagine, on that pristine summer day, the wrath in the Pacific waiting to be unleashed.

While I was kicking back on the beach, watching sets roll in from a Southern Hemisphere ground swell, a local TV news crew showed up to get some footage for an evening segment regarding El Niño—using Malibu as an ideal backdrop for their story. I talked with the weatherman, Paul Johnson as the crew set up their shoot. Paul and I talked briefly about the upcoming El Niño, which lead to a conversation regarding the conditions for the surfing competition held at Malibu that day.

Paul remarked on how flat the surf looked, and that this might not be an ideal day for the event. Within a minute of his remark, a sweet 4-foot set rolled through with competitors in the water hopping up, walking their boards and hanging ten. This local weatherman seemed a little stunned, not realizing that there was a long-period ground swell in the water and that he based his initial comment on his brief, immediate view, which was merely a lull-period between sets.

The fact is that we can't predict surfing conditions by merely running down to the beach, looking at the water, and getting a *feel* for what's going to happen later. We might be able to do this with the weather to a certain degree, at least for short-range forecasts, looking at the sky, and seeing if dark clouds are on the horizon. Even that would only give us a myopic prediction. Standing on the beach and looking out over the water our horizon is limited to about 3 miles[1]; hardly enough distance to predict surfing conditions.

To predict swells, winds, and other conditions accurately, we need to see what's happening across the oceans. If we had excellent vision, instead of standing on the beach and viewing our limited horizon, we could climb to a higher elevation, and extend our observation; thereby, seeing even more of the ocean to judge incoming conditions. But we'd need to get up pretty high and have tremendous powers of sight to see the activity on the ocean that would bring us surf.

In fact, events that occur thousands of miles away affect our surf days later. Thanks to the advancement of science and technology, we can visually see what's occurring on the entire ocean surface in the way of winds, swell heights, and other data that's useful to surf forecasting. Satellites and other various means of analysis gather information on recent ocean events that forecasting computers crunch into a visual representation of what is happening on the open sea. These representations are called models.

Models give you a "bird's eye view" (actually a view from space) of the ocean events, representing not only the present conditions, but also the forecasted conditions for at least the next few days. What's even better is that most of these models are free to the public. You can access these models on the Internet, and make use of the information they contain to forecast surf for your favorite breaks.

Models play a vital role in forecasting surf conditions. However, that is typically not the intention for many of the models generated today. For the most part, models showing open ocean systems are primarily intended for the maritime industries and naval interests. Mariners use these models to track storms on the open ocean, warning of impending danger days ahead of time. Still, as we'll see

---

1.   This is referring to surface horizon. Mountains, islands and the like are at higher horizons, allowing for extended visibility.

later on, we will be using these same models to track incoming swell energy to our coast.

Models are a science unto themselves. There is a lot of work that goes into making the models, and the systems that generate them. Geared towards the science and maritime communities, these models may be foreign to you. If you're not familiar with reading models, I think you'll find this chapter very useful, preparing you for many topics we'll be covering throughout this book. Models may seem confusing at first, but they're straightforward once you learn some of the basics.

In this chapter, we'll look at the most popular model, the Wave Analysis Model, also called a WAM. All of the WAM's illustrated throughout this book are free to the public and, I've listed links to some great resources containing these WAM's in the "Resources" chapter near the end of this book.

After discussing the features of these models, we'll also briefly discuss some idiosyncrasies of these "flat" looking models that are representing our spherical planet.

First, let's look at the most common model we'll be using, the Wave Analysis Model (WAM), shown in Figure 2. This particular WAM is showing us significant wave heights in the Pacific, but there are WAM's that cover the entire globe.

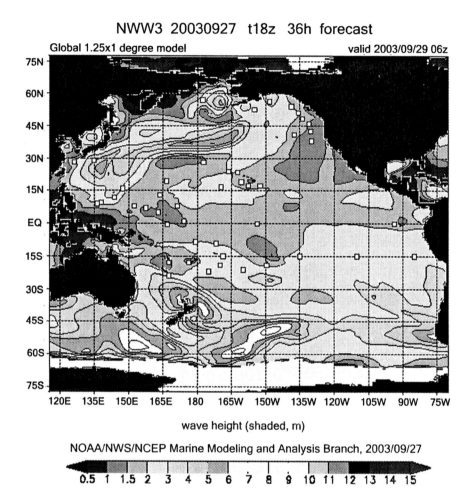

NWW3 20030927 t18z 36h forecast

Figure 2 Wave Model Example

As mentioned earlier, I apologize for the black and white image; when you look at these on the Internet they are in color. Nevertheless, from this example we can still learn the basics of the wave analysis models.

Models display not only the current state, but also forecasts for the next few days. To cover this span of time, a series of models are generated during a "model run". This collection consists of many models, each representing a specific time in the future. The first model in the model run usually represents the time that the model run began. Then subsequent models are made using an increment of 6 to 12 hours. So in a model run, you'll see models for 0 hour (current), then models for a 12 hour projection, 24 hour projection, 36 hour projection, etc., running as high as 168 hours into the future.

We can see a model run that the example WAM in Figure 2 was part of from the Marine Modeling and Analysis Branch of NOAA web site at http://polar.wwb.noaa.gov/waves/main_text.html. There you'll see lists of models like these:

- **Atlantic   Ocean   from   global   model   Hs** : animation, -6h, 0h, 6h, 12h, 18h, 24h, 30h, 36h, 42h, 48h, 54h, 60h, 66h, 72h, 78h, 84h, 90h, 96h, 102h, 108h, 114h, 120h, 126h, 132h, 138h, 144h, 150h, 156h, 162h, 168h

- **Pacific   Ocean   from   global   model   Tp** : animation, -6h, 0h, 6h, 12h, 18h, 24h, 30h, 36h, 42h, 48h, 54h, 60h, 66h, 72h, 78h, 84h, 90h, 96h, 102h, 108h, 114h, 120h, 126h, 132h, 138h, 144h, 150h, 156h, 162h, 168h

- **Pacific   Ocean   from   global   model   U10** : animation, -6h, 0h, 6h, 12h, 18h, 24h, 30h, 36h, 42h, 48h, 54h, 60h, 66h, 72h, 78h, 84h, 90h, 96h, 102h, 108h, 114h, 120h, 126h, 132h, 138h, 144h, 150h, 156h, 162h, 168h

The underlined texts (i.e. 0h, 6h, 12h, etc.) are hyperlinks that when clicked on, will show you that model. Note that there are numerous individual models, one for every 6 hours. The 0h model is the model showing the current analysis. -6h is a hindcast, showing what occurred 6 hours ago. The 6h, 12h, 18h, etc., are models that show forecast predictions (6 hours from now, 12 hours from now, 18 hours from now, etc.).

As with any forecast, the further out the prediction, the looser the tolerance for accuracy. In other words, from a model run, the 0h and 12h models have more accuracy to them than the 144h or 168h model.

Let's take a closer look at our example model in Figure 2 and dissect its important features. Starting from the top of this model, we get some critical information. All models will show you the time and day they were created, and the time and day they represent. In our example WAM, we can see that the model was created on September 27, 2003 (20030927).

Next, we see what time this model was created (t18Z) and that it's a 36-hour forecast (36h). This model also calculates out the forecast date and time for us (valid 2003/09/29 06z).

Note the Z in the time information. This stands for "Zulu" time, also known as GMT (Greenwich Mean Time) or UTC (Universal Time Coordinate). This is the time at the zero degree meridian crossing through Greenwich, England. GMT became a world time and date standard used by Britain's Royal Navy and merchant fleet during the nineteenth century, and it's still used today by the naval fleets and maritime industries worldwide. You'll find that practically all models use GMT time.

Converting GMT is not difficult, but can vary by one hour depending on Daylight Savings Time. I'll explain a quick rule of thumb to use on this, but if you want to get accurate, here's how you do the conversion for the US mainland coasts:

- GMT to EST = GMT - 5 hours
- GMT to EDT = GMT - 4 hours
- GMT to PST = GMT - 8 hours
- GMT to PDT = GMT - 7 hours
- GMT to HST = GMT - 10 hours

You can also see the times around the world at the *Time and Date* web site: http://www.timeanddate.com/worldclock/

So from our example WAM, we can see that for the west coast of the United States, the model was made on:

- Sep. 27, 2003 18Z - 7 hours = Sep. 27, 2003 11:00 AM PDT

From this, we can see what time this forecast is representing:

- Sep. 27, 2003 11:00 AM PDT + 36 hours = Sep. 28, 2003 11:00 PM

We could have also calculated the time for the US west coast from the supplied "valid" date and time on the model:

- 2003/09/29 06z - 7 hours = Sep. 28, 2003 11:00 PM

Note however that not all models are as forgiving, and many only supply the date and time that the model was created, and its forecast hour.

As I mentioned, this is the *exact* time conversion. However, there is a simple way to approach this. First, know what your local time difference is to GMT. Then grab models forecasted for the early morning and late afternoon hours. After a while, you'll become accustomed to figuring out only two model times for each day, making this conversion less painful.

Well, the hard part is over. The rest of the model is much easier. Despite the black and white image, we can still see that there are various colors on this model. Each color on a WAM portrays a different swell height on the ocean. A bar under the image shows the scale that is used. This scale is common to most models. The WAM in Figure 2 displays the swell height, also referred to as the significant wave height, in meters. Some models, as we'll see later on, represent swell periods, but use a similar colored bar as their reference key.

Also, note that some models use feet instead of meters. To ensure your accuracy when making calculations based on these models, always look at the colored bar to see the reference units used for this key.

The WAM also shows the coordinate system. On our example model, there are longitude coordinates on the bottom, representing the longitudinal lines running from top to bottom of the grid. The left side has the latitude coordinates for the lines running left to right. These coordinates play a crucial role in the forecast calculations we'll encounter throughout this book. We'll look at this coordinate system in more detail in the next chapter, "Basic Geography".

It is important to note that the models we'll be using throughout this book, like that in Figure 2, represent the world as being flat. This is known as a Mercator projection. A Mercator projection is a mathematical method of showing a map of the globe on a flat surface, originally developed by Gerhardus Mercator, a Flemish geographer, in 1568. Before this time, navigation charts used by sailors did not correctly account for the fact that the world is round.

But since the world is round, the Mercator projection is a distorted view of the Earth. On a globe, the lines of longitude converge at the poles and the lines of latitude are equidistant. This is shown in Figure 3, where we can see a how the lines of longitude are in fact curved, and converge at the poles.

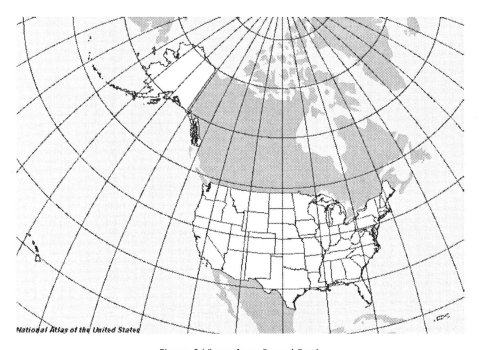

Figure 3 View of our Round Earth

This orthographic view provided by *National Atlas of the United States®*[2] shows how the lines of longitude are not equally spaced as you travel away from the equator to the poles. If we were to look at a Mercator projection model, and factor in the curvature of the earth when tracking a storm, we would see a curved path like those shown in Figure 4. These are known as "great circle" paths.

---

2.   National Atlas of the United States® can be accessed on the web at
     http://nationalatlas.gov/. Please see Reference section for more information.

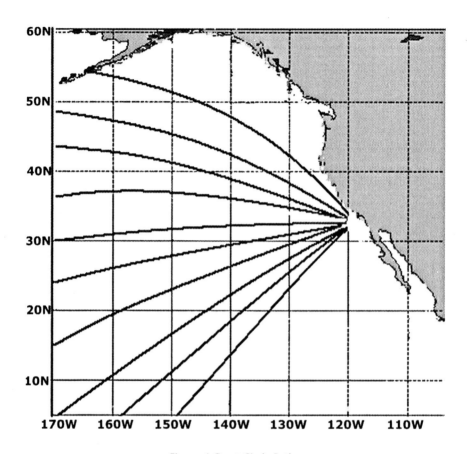

Figure 4 Great Circle Paths

The term "great circle" means we are looking at how this would be on a sphere. As we can see from this example diagram showing great circle paths from California, the actual path that a storm (or a ship) would take on a direct course across the globe would look somewhat curved, with the greatest curvature occurring at greater latitudes.

We'll discuss this anomaly of the models later when we cover the basics of predicting when swells will hit in Chapter 6, and look at easy ways to work around it.

For now, let's quickly cover some basic geography.

3

Basic Geography

○ ○

"The sea, washing the equator and the poles, offers its perilous aid, and the power and empire that follow it...'Beware of me,' it says, 'but if you can hold me, I am the key to all the lands.'"

—Ralph Waldo Emerson, The Conduct of Life, Wealth, 1860

Before getting down to the nitty gritty of surf forecasting, I'd like to divert your attention for just a moment to some geographical basics. In this chapter, we'll be taking a brief look at some lesser-known regions, mostly across the Pacific, that are often referred to in the WaveCast® reports, and mentioned at various times throughout this book. We'll also look at the coordinate system of the Earth and briefly discuss angle interpretation.

Knowing these simple basics will help you track the systems that we talk about in our free online forecasts and examples in this book, and possibly broaden your knowledge of common swell origination locales.

Figure 5 illustrates two of the three subjects that we'll be covering in this chapter: geographic points of interest, and the world coordinate system.

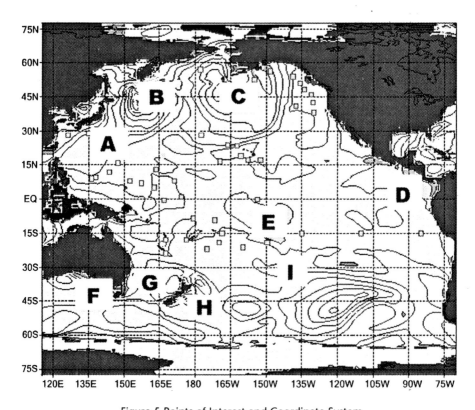

Figure 5 Points of Interest and Coordinate System

Figure 5 is a modified version of a NOAA WAM, similar to those we'll be using in a variety of examples. This WAM shows the world coordinate system that's used worldwide, like in GPS systems, to depict the exact location of anyone, place or thing. In the case of surf forecasting, these coordinates play a crucial role in tracking our incoming swells.

The lines that run vertically are longitude coordinates. The horizontal lines are latitude coordinates. The Equator is the center of the latitude coordinate system. This separates the Southern Hemisphere (below the equator) from the Northern Hemisphere (above the equator). Latitude coordinates in the Southern Hemisphere have an S after them, while the Northern Hemisphere coordinates use an N.

Similarly, the longitude coordinates are divided as well. In this case, at 180 degrees, the International Date Line separates the Eastern Hemisphere from the Western Hemisphere with E and W letters following their respective coordinates.

Knowing the world coordinate system is straightforward, and all of the examples in this book will show this coordinate system as well. In our examples, we might refer to a coordinate of 30S, 140W. This would be close to the point labeled "I" on this map (near Tahiti).

It's also important to note that our example map in Figure 5 was showing the Pacific view. Figure 6 shows an Atlantic view.

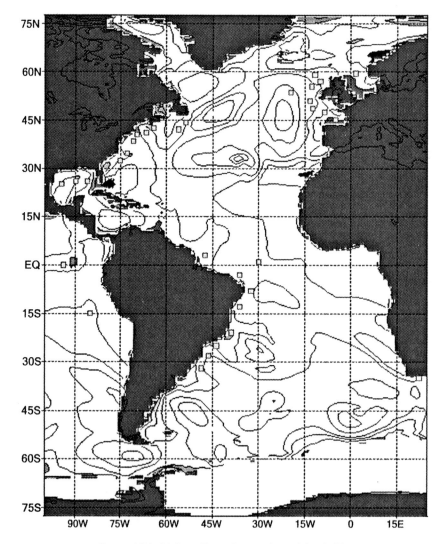

Figure 6 World Coordinate System from Atlantic View

Notice the zero longitude coordinate. This is known as the "Prime Meridian", which runs through Greenwich England (where GMT is referenced).

Being smaller than the Pacific, the Atlantic and other oceans around the world have geographic regions that most of us are familiar with, at least if you surf the coastal waters of those areas. However, since the Pacific is so vast, it has many more swell-generating regions, including some you may not be familiar with. For this reason, I thought it would be best to limit our discussion on geographic points of interest to the Pacific Ocean, illustrated in Figure 5.

The points of interest shown in Figure 5 are:

- **A: Japan:** During big winters, we'll reference storms moving across from this location towards Hawaii and the west coast of the US. Sometimes during the summer, typhoons will form in this region and move towards the Gulf of Alaska, bringing unseasonable northwest swell to the west coast of the US.

- **B: Kamchatka Peninsula:** This is right next to the Bering Sea, and is a prime location for wintertime northwest swells to form.

- **C: Aleutian Chain:** We reference this location constantly in our US west coast reports. Once storms coming from the Western Pacific cross this line, all heads are up on the west coast of the US as surf is imminent in a matter of days.

- **D: Costa Rica, Eastern Equatorial Pacific:** This is a prime location for hurricanes and tropical disturbances to form, giving surf mostly for Southern California and Baja. Note that tropical disturbances tend to form at or above 15N.

- **E: Christmas Island:** Santa Claus doesn't live here, but when a southern hemi swell passes this area, a buoy located near this island gives a solid indicator of how much energy is heading northward.

- **F: Australia and Southern Ocean:** Besides being the famous land down under, we can watch storms down under this outback continent in the Southern Ocean. Storms tend to form in the Southern Ocean, and glide easterly towards New Zealand (see H).

- **G: Tasman Sea:** This sea, located between Australia and New Zealand, is a tricky place for swells aimed at the west coast of the US and Hawaii. Right above this region are numerous islands, which tend to soak up much of the swell energy generated by systems that travel northward from the Southern Ocean into this region.

- **H: New Zealand (to the left of H):** This is the most common place where south swells form that bring surf to the west coast of the US during the Northern Hemisphere summer.

- **I: Tahiti:** This is also a common place for Southern Hemisphere swells to form, and works as a good indicator prior to the Christmas Island region.

The last subject of this chapter is what we call angle interpretation. When we talk about swells and wind, we reference an angle that they are coming from. These angles refer to those shown in Figure 7.

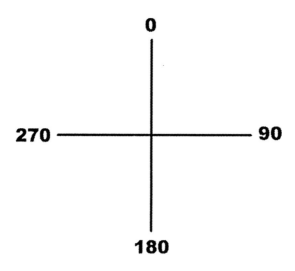

Figure 7 Angle Reference

When we say that a swell is coming in from 90 degrees, this means the swell is coming in from the east. If we say the swell is coming in from 180 degrees, the swell is coming in from the south. If the swell were coming in from 210, this would be southwest.

Now that we know some wave anatomy, model basics, geographic points of interest, the world coordinate system, and angles, it's time to dive in and see how waves are created.

4

The Origin of Waves

"I really don't know why it is that all of us are so committed to the sea, except I think it's because in addition to the fact that the sea changes, and the light changes, and ships change, it's because we all came from the sea. And it is an interesting biological fact that all of us have, in our veins the exact same percentage of salt in our blood that exists in the ocean, and therefore, we have salt in our blood, in our sweat, in our tears. We are tied to the ocean. And when we go back to the sea—whether it is to sail or to watch it—we are going back from whence we came."

—John F. Kennedy

You're standing on the beach, watching a nice set roll in. On the horizon, you watch bulges rise from the still, flat surface of the water, slowly rolling towards land. On their approach these incipient waves get sharper, rising slightly upwards, until finally this swelling of water becomes too thin and starts to break. Water, once blue now turns white with foam, peeling along as the wave continues to break. You can hear the thundering crash of this breaking wave, sensing its energy, knowing you are about to go up against it and become one with this incoming force.

But where did this energy come from? What made the flat ocean surface on the horizon rise, sharpen, then crash with such strength? From our perspective, standing on the beach, we can only see a fraction of the ocean from where these waves originated. However, if we were looking from space, it would appear as though someone dropped a rock in the ocean, and ripples traveled out from its initial splash.

In a sense, that's really the essence of ocean wave origination. Something disturbed the ocean surface similar to a pebble tossed into a pond of water. However, in the case of ocean waves, a pebble didn't make the initial splash. Instead, it was most likely from a storm that formed thousands of miles away, or it could be from a local disturbance in coastal waters. In most cases wind, and lots of it, creates the waves that we surf.

There are three primary types of ocean waves[1]. The most uncommon are Tsunami waves typically generated by earthquakes. Also known as tidal waves, it is rare that we would ever surf these. The more common types of waves we see are known as ground swell waves, and wind swell waves.

A ground swell, despite its implied name, is caused by wind, just like its choppier cousin: wind swell. Ground swells typically form at least a thousand miles away from our shores. Massive storms on the high seas drive intense winds that disturb the ocean surface and create waves that we see days later.

Wind swells on the other hand form fairly close to shore. Still, like the ground swells, wind transferred energy into the water. The water reacted by creating waves. Wind swells are created by winds blowing close to shore (hundreds of miles or less), and ground swells are created by winds blowing far away from shore (usually 1000 miles or more, sometimes a little less).

This concept, of winds generating waves, goes way back to the ancient Greeks. Aristotle realized that wind on the sea surface played a vital role in wave development. But the physics to explain the energy transfer from wind to waves was a long ways away. Today however, we have the answers.

Since Aristotle's early studies, numerous scientists have honed the science of ocean dynamics so we can see the results of wind to wave energy transfer. Today we can watch the formation of ground swells and wind swells using WAM's. Figure 8 shows a WAM that illustrates a ground swell generating system.

---

1.   For this discussion, we'll cover these three. Scientifically speaking, there are capillary, chop, swell, seiche, tsunami, and shallow waves.

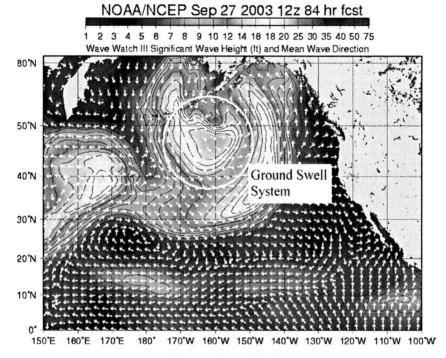

Figure 8 Ground Swell

In this example, a storm with intense winds caused a large disturbance under the Aleutian Chain. This particular storm was located about 1800 miles away from the California coast, a fair distance for a ground swell—enough to bring in some decent surf to California beaches. In fact, this particular ground-swell-generating system brought 6–8 foot surf to Northern California a few days later.

WAM's can also show us wind swells in the same manner as the ground swell shown in Figure 8. The only difference is the location of the storm creating the swell. A wind swell would be located very close to the coast, and a ground swell would be located very far away (like the one in Figure 8).

In both cases—ground swells and wind swells—wind created what's called fetch. Fetch is the area that the wind blows over the ocean surface without changing direction. Figure 8 has a circle around the fetch created by a very windy storm system. Strong wind was sustained for a long enough period of time in a constant direction to create this fetch.

Fetch is what we use to track swells. Comparing this to the "pebble and the pond" analogy, wind is like the pebble being tossed into a pond—it creates a disturbance. Fetch is a result of how hard the pebble was thrown (the wind speed), the size of the pebble that was thrown (duration of the wind), and at what angle the pebble was thrown (the direction of the wind). From this, we can derive swell strength, intensity, and direction. This information tells us how big waves will be, how long it will take them to arrive, and where they will travel to.

Our ground swell example shows a large amount of fetch with swell heights in the center of this disturbance running in the 20–25 foot range. If this system were close to shore, the coastline would get pummeled. However, this ground swell system formed at such a long distance from the California coast that this didn't happen.

Just like dropping that pebble in a pond of water, the outgoing ripples (in our case ocean waves) fade as they continue to spread. Energy dissipates as it travels away from its energy source and passes through mass (i.e. the ocean water and air) due to friction and other effects. In the case of ocean waves, this helps to do two things. First, the weaker waves, consisting of the choppy rough seas in the midst of the originating fetch will fade, provided the storm remains far away from the coast. The second result of the energy dissipation is that the strongest waves will make it through, albeit somewhat smaller because of the dissipation and other factors imposed on them through their distant journey to your coastline.

Figure 9 illustrates this concept:

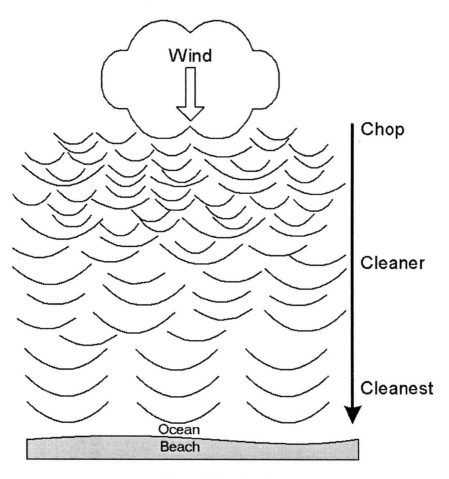

Figure 9 Wave Creation

As we can see from Figure 9, the farther away the swell-generating wind is, the cleaner the swell will be once it arrives. Distant ground swells end up with cleaner, long period waves. But in the case of close-proximity wind swell, the chop doesn't have as much time and distance to clean up, making for shorter periods and peakier conditions.

To summarize:

- Energy from wind out at sea is transferred into the ocean water.
- The water reacts by making wave energy.
- Wave energy will travel greatest in the direction that the wind is blowing.
- The stronger the wind, the more energy gets transferred.
- Big energy means big waves. Small energy means small waves.
- The farther away the wind disturbance is located, the better chance we have at seeing cleaner waves (ground swell).
- The closer to the coast that waves are created, the choppier the conditions (wind swell).

It's also important to know that larger waves travel faster than smaller waves. If we dropped that pebble in a pond of water and watched it in slow motion, we would see the larger ripples (waves) reach the shores first. Then, the smaller waves would come in later. This order of wave travel is due to a factor called "wave dispersion" which sorts out the waves before they get to your beach. You see this as a swell fades away. The first day the swell arrives, you might have 3–5 foot surf. Then the next day the swell fades, and you have 2–3 foot surf.

The bigger waves were like the strongest runners in a marathon. The bigger waves came out ahead at the end of the race towards shore. The weaker ones got left behind, and came in last. Also, note that there are groups of marathon runners, known as "wave groups"—what we know as sets. As the waves leave the fetch created by the wind far out at sea, all of the various waves, great and small, form a continuous procession known as a "wave train". Over time, waves that are moving at the same speed (and subsequently the same approximate size) in this train will group together. Therefore, we not only have a period of time between waves (the wave or swell period), but also a period of time between groups of waves (the lull time between sets).

Throughout this book, we'll be looking at the biggest waves of a storm's fetch, since they will typically be the first to arrive. The measurement of the biggest waves in a fetch is referred to as the "significant wave height". We'll use calculations to determine how long these *significant* waves will take to get to your break, and how big they'll be once they arrive.

There is one other vital characteristic of waves, size, and their related energy to note before moving forward. We know that the harder the wind blows, the bigger the waves that are generated. But this also increases the space between the waves: the wave period. Therefore, bigger waves tend to have longer periods. Smaller waves tend to have shorter periods. A ground swell may have 16 to 20 second periods that could bring in, say 6–8 foot surf. A wind swell on the other hand may have only 8 to 10 second periods, which may bring in only 2–3 foot surf. We'll look at wave size calculations more in Chapter 7 and use periods as a means to gauge incoming wave size. Also, since big waves travel faster than smaller ones, and these bigger waves tend to have longer periods, we'll be using the wave periods in timing calculations as well.

Since we know that winds, and storms related to them are the creators of our surf, we can forecast when the waves will arrive, and how big they will be by tracking wind and storms across the ocean. We'll use these basics throughout the next few chapters to see how this is done.

Now let's explore what created these waves: wind.

5

Winds

The three great elemental sounds in nature are the sound of rain, the sound of wind in a primeval wood, and the sound of the outer ocean on a beach. I have heard them all, and of the three elemental voices, that of ocean is the most awesome, beautiful, and varied.

—Henry Beston

You get up early, drive down to the beach, and paddle out for your first session of the day. The water surface is smooth, glassy, and calm. After catching a few silky, lined-up waves, you notice a texture on the water's surface, and then lumps and bumps begin to form. Soon you feel the winds begin to pick up. Moments later those clean lines you were taking off on are now breaking harder, and not keeping their face for near as long. An invisible force, wind, is the culprit.

Winds play a vital role in water sports. We talked briefly in Chapter 4 how large swells are made on the open ocean from storms having massive winds. Wind can also create some localized choppier surf along your coast. Additionally, wind contributes to the quality of our sessions, making it glassy, rough, or blown out.

Understanding the creation of wind leads to a better understanding of how we can predict this imperceptible force of nature for three primary reasons:

1. Knowing how winds form helps you to understand the basis of surf forecasting. Remember that wind is the ultimate creator of ground and wind swells as wind merely transfers energy into the water, which results in waves that form hundreds or thousands of miles away.

2. You'll be able to predict local surface winds to make the most of the day—knowing if you'll be hitting pure glass, or will be tossed around in a "victory at sea" session.

3. Warning signs of possible anomalies such as upwelling or coastal eddies will become apparent.

In this chapter, we'll look at how winds form, the variables associated with winds, and some easy ways to forecast them. We'll also look at common wind patterns, and some anomalies caused by them.

First, let's look at the biggest difference between the two most common types of wind that we face while in the water: onshore winds and offshore winds shown in Figure 10.

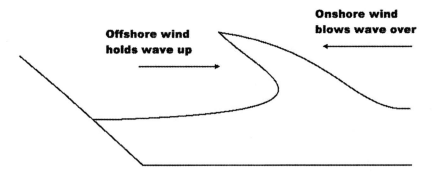

Figure 10 Offshore and Onshore Wind Effects

As shown, the wind usually does one of two things to breaking waves. If the wind is blowing onshore, it tends to blow the wave over as it builds, leaving less time for the wave face to rise and give a nice clean line to ride. Offshore winds on the other hand do just the opposite. These winds tend to hold the wave up as it builds, and somewhat slow it down. However, offshore winds, if strong enough, can also have adverse affects.

There are also slight variations of onshore and offshore winds known as side-shore winds that blow from different angles of onshore or offshore patterns. We can predict these patterns and other stronger winds at sea by looking at some science behind the winds. Understanding these first two basic patterns—onshore and offshore winds—will set the stage for further discussions on other types of wind affecting our sessions and swells.

No matter what the wind pattern, pressure and temperature differences associated with the atmosphere create winds. The atmosphere around us is comprised of high-pressure areas, and low-pressure areas. High pressure, as its name implies, is an area of pressure that is greater than normal. High-pressure near the Earth's surface is where heavier air slowly descends, due to its denser properties. Low-pressure is just the opposite, and has lighter air that rises from the Earth's surface. In both cases, the descending air of high pressure and rising air of low-pressure travel at speeds that are, for the most part, unnoticeable to the naked eye. Their progression is typically quite slow.

Descending air in a high-pressure area warms up as it falls through the atmosphere, which hinders the formation of clouds. This is why blue skies and clear weather are associated with high-pressure systems.

Low pressure is just the opposite. Air in a low-pressure system rises since it has very little weight. As air rises, it also cools, picking up humidity on the way like a cool glass of water in a humid room on a hot summer day. As this rising air continually gathers moisture, clouds form which in turn can create storm systems.

Both high and low-pressure systems intertwine in a symbiotic bond. The falling air in a high-pressure system had to get its air from somewhere. Rising air from low pressure is the one to thank for that. As air rises in one low-pressure area, it will eventually descend in a high-pressure area.

In a low-pressure system, rising air pulls in air from around it, creating winds. In a high-pressure system, the falling air can help to push the wind. This is shown in Figures 11 and 12.

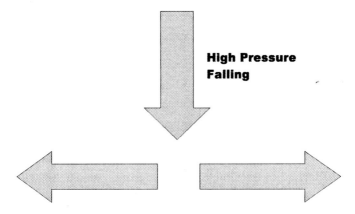

Figure 11 High Pressure Falling Pushes Wind

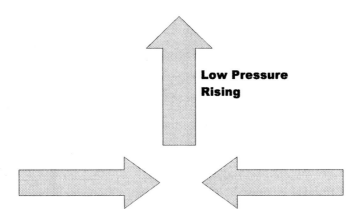

Figure 12 Low Pressure Pulling Winds

The difference in pressure between a high-pressure system and a low-pressure system will determine the wind's speed. The greater the difference between low and high pressure, the greater the pull and/or push of the air will be. This pressure difference is the most important variable in forecasting wind. Even if the low has very low pressure, it takes a high with a very large difference in pressure from the low to create strong wind.

To see a simple example of how pressure differences affect wind, let's look at the most common type of wind we encounter while we're in the water: the onshore sea breeze pattern we previously discussed. This pattern is illustrated in Figure 13.

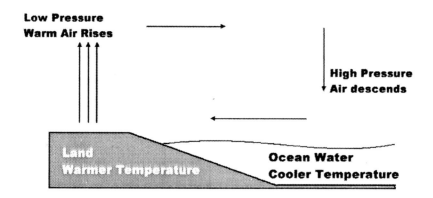

Figure 13 Sea breeze Pattern

In the onshore sea breeze pattern, warm air rises off the land, sucking in heavier air over the ocean surface. The warmer the land mass, the greater the low pressure compared to that over the cooler ocean waters. This results in a pressure difference between the land and the ocean. In the case of the onshore sea breeze pattern, the greater the temperature difference, the greater the difference in pressure will be. The warmer the land becomes, the lower the pressure, resulting in faster acceleration of rising air in the low pressure area, which in turn causes a faster pull on the air moving in from the ocean. Hence, the lower the pressure over land in comparison to the higher pressure over the water, the stronger the winds.

This explains why so many surf spots will have calm winds in the morning when the land mass is relatively cool. Then in the afternoon, when the land mass is warmer, the air over land rises more quickly, resulting in a stronger sea breeze, and the possibility for blown-out conditions.

Note that the sea breeze example shows a small-scaled version of winds from pressure differences, known quite often as a "diurnal" pattern (pattern occurring regularly during a day). Still, it was a difference in pressure—low pressure over land, high pressure over the ocean—that caused the wind to blow from the ocean to land.

Offshore winds, like California's Santa Ana winds, are just the opposite of an onshore sea breeze, making them an ideal topic to explain the offshore pattern. Santa Ana winds can wreak havoc due to their extremely strong nature, well noted during the infamous wild fires in late October 2003 in Southern California. However, if these winds are calm to moderate, they can bring some pristine offshore conditions.

Like all winds, Santa Ana's are created by a pressure differential. However, the location of the high and low-pressure systems is the opposite of the onshore sea breeze pattern. In the Santa Ana offshore scenario, high pressure strengthens inland, typically over the "Great Basin" near Idaho and the Salt Lake. As this heavier air descends onto the high-elevation desert regions, it gets sucked across the land from a low-pressure system located off the coast of California. As these winds get pulled across land, they funnel through canyons and other natural landmasses that act as amplifiers of the wind energy. Not originating from the ocean, these winds have little to no moisture, causing very dry and often quite warm conditions.

For the most part, all winds are created the same way: by a difference in pressure. Even the ever-popular trade winds that blow through many tropical regions like Hawaii are created by pressure differences. Albeit the pressure difference causing the trade winds is from large bands of pressure known as the subtropical high and a low known as the Intertropical Convergence Zone. Still, when it comes to forecasting winds, pressure difference is the key.

This similarity in wind formation (from pressure differences) allows us to forecast winds, no matter what the region. However, it is important to note that each area typically has a distinctive pattern to its winds, making it unique. With practice of forecasting wind for your area, and confirming it with local readings (which we'll get to shortly), you'll become accustomed to the various winds for your favorite spots, and know how pressure systems will affect them.

As mentioned, winds are also important to understanding the formation of storm systems on the open ocean that can bring us surf. Wind transfers energy into the water which later results in waves on our shores. In both cases of wind prediction, for either coastal conditions, or tracking swell generating winds, forecasting techniques remain pretty much the same. It's simply a matter of tracking the *difference* in pressure across a given area.

The difference in pressure is called a "pressure gradient", often referred to as "grads". To see the grads, as well as other wind information, we can use pressure maps, such as the one in Figure 14 provided by the California Regional Weather server at http://virga.sfsu.edu/

Figure 14 Pressure Map

There are four points of interest on this map:

- **Isobars:** These are the circular, curvy shaped lines. These represent the pressure, and the pressure difference (gradients).

- **Wind Barbs**: These look like little keys, and show us wind direction and speed. Not all pressure maps have wind barbs, but wind speed and direction can be calculated just the same.

- **Low Pressure Center**: This is designated by the letter L

- **High Pressure Center**: This is designated by the letter H

If you look closely at this pressure map, you can see a few additional items. Notice the outline of the west coast of the US, Canada, and Alaska. Also, note that there is a low-pressure center located right under the Aleutian Chain near the Gulf of Alaska, and a high-pressure center near the bottom center of the map, west of Baja.

It's important to note that this pressure map is representing sea level readings (often referred to as 4mb). Many pressure maps are available for 300mb and 500mb readings measured in the troposphere, far above the Earth's surface. These higher-level readings tend to be much stronger than the surface measurements. So when looking at pressure maps for wind measurements, it's advisable to use sea level readings if possible.

The isobars give us the biggest clue on the winds. Isobars that are farther apart indicate calmer winds (a smaller gradient). Isobars that are closer together represent stronger winds (a larger gradient). The denser the isobars, the higher the gradients will be. Higher gradients mean stronger winds. Therefore, when you see isobars tightly packed, you're seeing an indicator of strong wind.

In our pressure map example, we can see some very tight isobars around the low-pressure system entering the Gulf of Alaska, indicating strong winds near those isobars. As such, you can also predict that waves are being generated as a result, which we'll discuss more in the next chapter. For our wind forecast however, we can see that there is a high likelihood of strong winds in the Gulf of Alaska region, and across the Aleutian Chain. However, for the west coast of America, these winds would me much less, confirmed by the looser isobars along the California coast.

Winds tend to flow parallel to the isobars. In the Northern Hemisphere, winds blow counterclockwise around a low-pressure system and clockwise around a high-pressure system. This is the opposite in the Southern Hemisphere, due to the Coriolis Effect, a force of nature due to the Earth's rotation and curvature.

In our pressure map, we would expect winds to be strong and from a southerly direction onto the southern coast of Alaska. We can deduce this by the tight isobars around the low showing winds that would parallel these dense lines and rotate counterclockwise (south to north) around the low-pressure system. The wind barbs confirm this as well.

The wind barbs show us the direction and speed of the wind. The direction the barb is facing tells us where the wind is coming from, as shown in Figure 15.

Wind Direction

Figure 15 Wind Barb

The wind barbs also tell us the wind speed. The more "barbs", the stronger the winds, as shown in Figure 16.

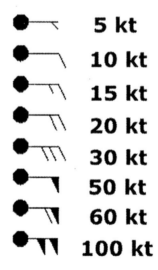

Figure 16 Wind Barb Table

Each "barb" on a wind barb represents 10 knots (about 11.5 mph). A half barb represents only 5 knots. A pendant (flag) represents 50 knots.

If the pressure maps you're accessing don't have wind barbs, you can still calculate the amount of wind by the spacing of the isobars using Table B-1 in Appendix B.

As we can see from our pressure map, there are stronger winds swirling around the low-pressure system hitting the Gulf Coast of Alaska than there are near the California coast.

Also, notice how the wind trend along the California coast appears to be somewhat offshore, especially in Southern California. Remember that high-pressure systems rotate clockwise in the Northern Hemisphere. Since Southern California and Baja are located near the high pressure, the winds are circulating in the opposite direction than the low that is centered under the Aleutians.

Now let's look at this same scenario a week later. Our example pressure map in Figure 14 is from Sep. 30 at 12z (5 AM PDT). Our next example in Figure 17 is from Oct. 7 at the same time of the day.

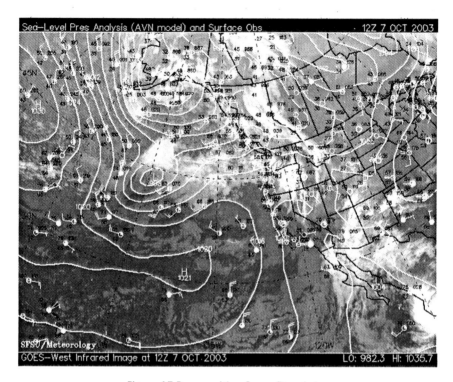

Figure 17 Pressure Map Seven Days Later

From our previous pressure map to this one, (over a span of 7 days) we can see that the low has moved eastward. Isobars from the low are now pointing more towards Northern California and areas farther to the north.

The low-pressure system in Figure 17 is swirling counterclockwise off the Oregon coast, in the Gulf of Alaska. This is swirling winds toward the coasts of Washington, Oregon, and Northern California. We can also see that the high-pressure system located far below the low-pressure system would be swirling very light winds in a clockwise direction, bringing some slight offshore conditions to Southern California and Baja.

I realize the wind barbs are difficult to see on this pressure map and, there is a better way to get the current wind data. To see winds closer and more accurate to your forecast area, you may want to turn to buoys for some real-time information. Buoys are a great source for short-range wind forecasts. The National Data Buoy Center, located at http://www.ndbc.noaa.gov/ has links to buoys all over the US, Caribbean, and parts of Europe. Many countries have buoy networks in place as well, some of which are listed in the "Resources" chapter near the end of this book. Buoys provide great indicators of the current and latest winds from the past day or so. The NDBC buoy readings are typically taken every hour, allowing you to see trends in the winds.

Let's look at the winds along the California coast at the time of our 7-day example on Oct. 7. A report from Buoy Station 46011 located 21 nautical miles northwest of Point Arguello, California for Oct. 7 is shown in Figure 18.

Previous 24 observations

MM DD	HH PDT	WDIR	WSPD kts	GST kts	WVHT ft	DPD sec	APD sec	MWD	PRES in	PTDY in	ATMP °F	WTMP °F
10 07	12 pm	NW	9.7	13.6	7.5	14	7.0	-	29.83	+0.00	55.0	56.7
10 07	11 am	NNW	9.7	13.6	7.2	17	6.7	-	29.83	+0.02	55.0	56.7
10 07	10 am	NNW	11.7	15.5	7.9	17	6.9	-	29.83	+0.02	54.9	56.5
10 07	9 am	NNW	13.6	17.5	7.5	17	6.7	-	29.83	+0.02	54.7	56.7
10 07	8 am	NNW	9.7	13.6	8.2	8	6.8	-	29.81	+0.00	54.7	56.7
10 07	7 am	NW	11.7	13.6	8.2	8	6.7	-	29.81	+0.01	55.0	56.7
10 07	6 am	NNW	11.7	13.6	8.5	8	6.7	-	29.81	-0.00	54.9	56.7
10 07	5 am	NNW	13.6	17.5	7.9	17	6.8	-	29.81	-0.00	56.7	56.7
10 07	4 am	NNW	11.7	15.5	7.5	8	7.4	-	29.80	-0.02	57.4	56.7
10 07	3 am	NNW	9.7	11.7	7.9	17	7.6	-	29.81	-0.01	56.7	56.7
10 07	2 am	NNW	7.8	9.7	7.9	8	7.4	-	29.81	-0.02	56.5	56.7
10 07	1 am	N	5.8	7.8	6.9	8	6.9	-	29.82	-0.01	56.5	56.7
10 07	12 am	NNW	11.7	13.6	7.2	8	6.9	-	29.82	+0.00	56.7	56.7
10 06	11 pm	NW	13.6	15.5	7.2	8	6.7	-	29.83	+0.01	56.5	57.2
10 06	10 pm	NW	11.7	15.5	6.9	7	6.5	-	29.83	+0.03	57.4	57.4
10 06	9 pm	NW	11.7	15.5	6.9	8	6.3	-	29.83	+0.02	56.7	57.4
10 06	8 pm	NNW	11.7	13.6	7.2	8	6.3	-	29.81	-0.00	56.1	57.4
10 06	7 pm	NW	9.7	13.6	7.5	8	6.0	-	29.80	-0.01	55.9	57.4
10 06	6 pm	NW	13.6	15.5	7.5	7	6.2	-	29.80	-0.01	55.9	57.6
10 06	5 pm	NW	15.5	19.4	8.5	20	6.5	-	29.81	+0.00	56.1	57.6
10 06	4 pm	NW	9.7	13.6	7.9	20	6.4	-	29.81	-0.02	55.2	57.6
10 06	3 pm	NW	11.7	15.5	7.5	20	6.6	-	29.81	-0.04	55.2	57.6
10 06	2 pm	WNW	7.8	11.7	8.5	20	7.7	-	29.82	-0.04	55.2	57.4
10 06	1 pm	NW	9.7	13.6	6.6	20	6.5	-	29.83	-	54.9	57.4

Figure 18 Buoy Report Pt. Arguello, CA

As this example shows, you can get the wind readings for the past 24 hours. The first few columns show the date and time of the reading. The fourth column shows the wind direction. The fifth column shows the wind speed that is sustained (a steady wind). And the sixth column shows the speed of wind gusts. Note also that you can see the wave heights at this buoy in the seventh column, and dominant wave period (DPD) in the eighth column. We'll talk more about getting "Now Casts" for the surf information in Chapter 13. But for now, we'll concentrate on the wind portions of the report.

By reading buoys up and down your coast, you can judge from the wind direction, and the location of the buoys, the potential for wind in your area. From this buoy, we can see that wind has been blowing steadily for the past 24 hours, although somewhat stronger around 9 and 10 AM. The wind blew all night as well. This tells us a few things.

First, we can feel confident that the winds will be near 10–14 kt, and not much less, in the short term near this buoy. Bear in mind however that this buoy is located 21 nautical miles off shore. The winds at this buoy will likely be stronger than winds closer to shore. The coastline bends and curves, creating wind breaks which act as wind barriers and filters. With some practice, you'll be able to tell from the wind at the buoys what to expect at your favorite surf spots.

Second, since this buoy is located north of Los Angeles, which is a basin prone to coastal eddies, the NW winds that have been blowing past this buoy are likely to blow down the coast, increasing the likelihood of a coastal eddy. However, these winds are somewhat light for eddy formation, but a weak eddy could still form. If you're not familiar with the coastal eddy weather phenomenon, you might want to check out some of the Internet links listed in the "Resources" chapter near the end of this book (see Coastal Eddy section).

Third, this steady wind from the NW that is paralleling the California coast could be an indicator of an upwelling that could affect water temperatures. We'll cover more on predicting upwelling and water temperature fluctuations in Chapter 15.

Now let's look at a buoy farther down the California coast. Remember, from our Point Arguello buoy, located north of LA, the winds are, and have been blowing from the NW. This means we can look at LA, and see how this could affect that region. Figure 19 shows a buoy report for station 46025 located 33 nautical miles WSW of Santa Monica.

Previous 24 observations

MM	DD	HH PDT	WDIR	WSPD kts	GST kts	WVHT ft	DPD sec	APD sec	MWD	PRES in	PTDY in	ATMP °F	WTMP °F
10	07	12 pm	WSW	5.8	7.8	3.9	9	7.2	-	29.82	+0.00	61.7	63.9
10	07	11 am	-	0.0	1.9	3.6	9	6.7	-	29.83	+0.02	62.6	64.0
10	07	10 am	-	0.0	1.9	3.9	8	7.1	-	29.83	+0.02	62.4	63.9
10	07	9 am	W	1.9	3.9	3.6	10	6.9	-	29.82	+0.03	61.7	63.7
10	07	8 am	-	0.0	1.9	3.3	9	6.7	-	29.81	+0.02	61.3	63.7
10	07	7 am	SSE	3.9	5.8	3.6	9	6.9	-	29.80	-0.00	61.0	63.5
10	07	6 am	SE	5.8	7.8	3.3	9	6.7	-	29.78	-0.02	60.8	63.5
10	07	5 am	E	5.8	7.8	3.6	10	6.9	-	29.78	-0.03	60.4	63.7
10	07	4 am	E	5.8	9.7	3.6	9	6.9	-	29.80	-0.01	60.1	64.8
10	07	3 am	SE	5.8	7.8	3.6	9	7.0	-	29.80	-0.01	59.9	65.5
10	07	2 am	E	5.8	9.7	3.6	8	6.8	-	29.81	-0.01	60.3	65.8
10	07	1 am	ESE	5.8	9.7	3.6	9	7.1	-	29.81	+0.00	60.8	65.8
10	07	12 am	SE	3.9	7.8	3.6	8	6.8	-	29.81	+0.01	61.5	65.8
10	06	11 pm	SSE	1.9	3.9	3.6	9	6.7	-	29.82	+0.02	61.5	65.8
10	06	10 pm	NW	1.9	5.8	3.3	9	6.6	-	29.81	+0.03	61.2	65.8
10	06	9 pm	NW	1.9	3.9	3.6	8	6.3	-	29.80	+0.02	61.2	66.0
10	06	8 pm	WNW	3.9	5.8	3.6	8	6.5	-	29.80	+0.01	61.2	66.0
10	06	7 pm	WNW	5.8	7.8	3.6	8	6.5	-	29.78	+0.00	61.7	66.0
10	06	6 pm	WNW	9.7	13.6	3.6	8	6.8	-	29.78	-0.01	61.2	66.4
10	06	5 pm	W	3.9	7.8	3.6	8	6.7	-	29.79	-0.02	61.3	66.4
10	06	4 pm	SSW	3.9	5.8	3.6	20	7.3	-	29.79	-0.04	61.0	65.5
10	06	3 pm	SSW	3.9	5.8	3.0	8	6.8	-	29.79	-0.06	60.8	65.5
10	06	2 pm	SW	5.8	5.8	3.3	8	6.7	-	29.81	-0.05	60.6	65.7
10	06	1 pm	SW	3.9	5.8	3.0	8	6.6	-	29.83	-	60.4	66.0

Figure 19 Buoy Report from LA

As we can see from this buoy, the winds have been much calmer. Judging from the past 24-hour comparison, it is unlikely that the NNW winds farther up the coast will have much effect. In fact, there will likely be glassy sessions in the morning.

This difference in winds from Central/Northern California (Point Arguello buoy) and Southern California (Santa Monica buoy) also coincides with the pressure map for the time of the buoy reports, (Oct. 7th) in Figure 17. Notice there are slightly stronger onshore winds in Northern California than there are in Southern California in both the pressure map and the buoy reports.

Although you can use buoys to see real time data, and forecast some downwind predictions, you can also turn to weather forecast models like those provided by the Fleet Numerical Meteorology and Oceanography Center (FNMOC) located at: https://www.fnmoc.navy.mil/. This site has a public access link where you can access weather models (WxMAP) as well as WAM's (WW3). Just like using WAM's, the weather models show projections of what is to occur over the next few days. You can see the atmospheric weather and wind patterns (300 heights, and 500 heights) or you can see the ocean surface winds.

Note that most of the WaveCast® reports at wetsand.com also provide you with a wind forecast chart, showing the expected winds over the next few days.

So now that we've discussed what makes the waves, and how wind can affect your sessions, it's time to forecast when swells will arrive based on their formation from wind far out at sea.

6

Knowing When

Knowing waves originate from strong winds out at sea, we can use various data to track the fetch created by these winds, and then calculate the arrival of the swell energy. Calculating the timing of a swell's arrival can be a challenge, and there's quite a bit of science behind it. Nevertheless, we'll look at the basics behind this science to understand what's involved, and I'll show you some simple methods to get a very close estimate of the swell arrival time.

After getting to know the "when" of forecasting, the following chapters will look at simple methods for wave size calculation, mitigating factors, tidal effects, seasonal effects, and other various topics. Then we'll compile all this knowledge into surf logs; a useful tool to quickly reference your forecast data, assemble a surf schedule, and learn how your surf spots work the swells you've been tracking. The first step however, is to know *when*.

As we discussed in the previous chapter on wind, we could tell by looking at pressure maps just how intense a low-pressure system and the gradients are. This could tell us the amount of wind in a storm system, which in turn, could be calculated into surf forecast data. For instance, we could calculate how much wind is associated with the low-pressure systems in the previous chapter. Then, from the locations of these lows, we could predict how long it would take the swell energy to arrive. From the strength of the winds, and the duration of time they were blowing, we could also calculate how big the waves would be.

There are two ways to approach this, depending on whether or not you have access to the Internet.

1. **If you don't have access to the Internet**, yet you do have access to pressure maps, then you can use the location and strength of the low-pressure systems for many of the calculations that we'll cover in this chapter (and the next chapter), using the tables in Appendix B.

2. **If you do have access to the Internet**, then there is a much easier method to derive fetch location and significant wave height using wave analysis models (WAM's).

In this chapter, we'll assume you do have Internet access, and can access the WAM's from the URL's provided in the "Resources" section of this book, or other similar models. Even if you don't have Internet access, and use the tables in Appendix B, much of what we'll discuss in this chapter and the following chapters will still apply.

As we discussed in Chapter 4, wind on the open sea creates fetch, which contains wave energy that eventually travels to the coastline. By tracking the fetch, we can calculate everything we need for swell arrival and size.

The surf-producing properties of a fetch are controlled by three primary factors:

1. Wind speed

2. Wind duration

3. Fetch size

Any one of these factors may limit or increase the wave height inside the fetch. If the wind speed is low, large waves are not produced, no matter how long the wind blows over an unlimited fetch. If the wind speed is great, but it blows for only a few minutes, no high waves are produced despite unlimited wind strength and fetch. On the other hand, if the wind is strong, and duration is long, then you'll have a large fetch with some big waves.

Performing fetch calculations by hand when tracking a storm can be tedious, and is why I prefer to use WAM's. As mentioned earlier, WAM's are generated using myriad weather and satellite data to calculate the current and near future state of the ocean's surface. These WAM's show us wave heights and other pertinent data on swells that are forming, ideally showing us a graphical representation of the fetch. WAM's do the hard work for you: calculating the fetch and its properties. Then all you have to do is look at the WAM's, and you can get all the data from the fetch that you'll need.

In this chapter, we'll be using WAM's to see where storms are brewing fetch on the high seas, and calculate from their positions how long it will take for swell to arrive.

Boiling down the most basic elements of swell arrival forecasting we need:

1. Location of the storm's fetch

2. Forecast location (i.e. your favorite surf spot)

3. Swell height inside the storm's fetch (max)

4. Swell period of the storm's fetch (max)

5. Direction that the storm, and its fetch, are traveling

To illustrate how these elements work together, we'll work through three examples, forecasting surf for the east coast of Florida, the west coast of Costa Rica, and Southern California. For each of these examples, we'll be using great circle calculations, which if you'll recall from Chapter 2 will take into account the curvature of the earth.

In our first example, we'll track a fairly large storm in Figure 20.

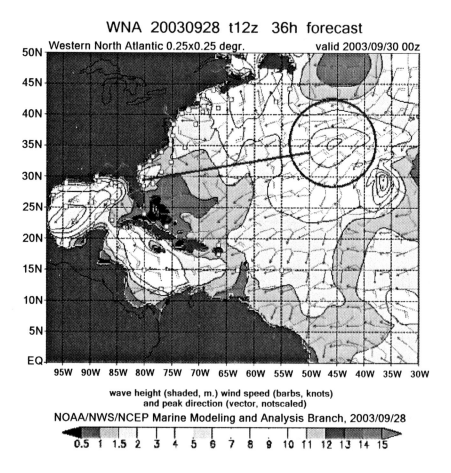

WNA 20030928 t12z 36h forecast

wave height (shaded, m.) wind speed (barbs, knots)
and peak direction (vector, notscaled)
NOAA/NWS/NCEP Marine Modeling and Analysis Branch, 2003/09/28

Figure 20 Example Swell for Florida

This example shows a storm forming in the northern mid Atlantic that could bring some surf to the east coast of the United States. For clarity, I've placed a circle around this storm's fetch, and have drawn a line from it to the Florida coast, which we'll use as our forecast location. We could also forecast this fetch for other areas of the east coast, since it would affect much of that region. But for this example, we'll keep it simple and use just one location: the east coast of Florida.

The location of this fetch has a leading edge at 35N, 50W. We can see this by the latitude coordinates on the left side of the graph (to get 35N) and the longitude coordinates on the bottom of the graph (to get 50W). The forecast location, on the east coast of Florida, is roughly at 27N, 80W.

The significant wave height, as shown by this model, is about 6 meters, or roughly 18 feet. This is difficult to determine from this black and white copy of the NOAA model, but the scale at the very bottom (running from 0.5 to 15) shows us how big the significant waves are in this fetch. This scale on the actual model is in color, making the wave height much easier to determine.

Although the significant wave height isn't necessary for the timing calculations that we'll cover in this chapter, it is still a vital piece of information to determine if this swell-making storm has enough power to produce surf potential. If the wave heights were only a few feet, swell would be less likely, and it may not be worthwhile to look at this system as a surf-generator. Although that's all we need to know for now, we will need the significant wave height for the size calculations that we'll use in the next chapter, "Knowing How Big".

We can see from the mean wave direction (the little arrows all over the model) that swell is pointing towards Florida. However, you can see that not all the arrows point directly at Florida as we approach the coastline. This, in a more accurate forecast, would need consideration, which we'll discuss in more detail in Chapter 8. For now, we'll assume the mean wave direction is pointing to our forecast area (Florida) which tells us that swell energy is heading that way.

We have a lot of information from this model, but it leaves out one important variable for our equation: the swell period. To see this, we need to look at a different type of model known as a "peak wave period" model. These models are available along with the significant height WAM's at the web sites listed in the "Resources" chapter near the end of this book. The WAM's we've looked at so far, showing significant wave height, are identified with an abbreviation "Hs". The peak wave period WAM's are usually abbreviated as "Tp".

The peak wave period model corresponding to the significant wave height WAM in Figure 20 is shown in Figure 21.

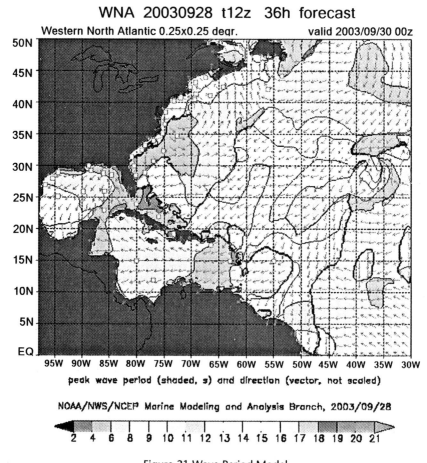

Figure 21 Wave Period Model

This peak wave period model shows us the primary periods between the waves, using the color scale at the bottom of the model as reference. At the location of our storm's fetch (35N, 50W) we have approximately 12-second periods.

With this information, we can begin the calculation for swell arrival time. Let's recap the information we have for this example swell:

- **Location of the fetch:** This storm's fetch has a leading edge at 35N, 50W.

- **Forecast Location**: For our example, we'll use a rough approximation to the east coast of Florida at 27N, 80W.

- **Swell height**: We know that the seas are about 18 feet, big enough to make this system worthwhile to track.

- **Swell period**: From the period model, we know there are 12-second periods where this storm is located, and from its leading edge pointed towards the Florida region.

- **Direction that the storm is traveling**: We can see from the mean wave direction arrows that the storm points directly towards Florida (at least close enough despite any great circle distortion).

Now we have enough information to calculate swell arrival time. A swell will move, on average, at a speed in nautical miles per hour (kt.) at approximately 1.5 times its period (actually about 1.515, but 1.5 is close enough). For instance, if you have a swell with 20-second periods, then it would travel at a speed of about 30 kt (20 * 1.5). If this swell were 3000 nautical miles away, it would take 3000/30= 100 hours to arrive (4.2 days). This gives us a formula of:

hours to arrive = (distance in nautical miles)/(period * 1.5)

Once we know how many nautical miles away the storm's fetch is from our forecast area, the calculation is easy. However, getting an accurate measurement in nautical miles can be tricky. As mentioned in Chapter 2, when we discussed the Mercator projection versus great circle measurements, the Earth is curved, and the models that we're looking at are flat. To make the great circle distance calculations easier, we provide, among other things at the WaveCast® web site, an on-line calculator at http://wavecast.com/guide . Using this calculator, you merely plug in the coordinates of the fetch and forecast locations, as well as the swell period. Our great circle calculator will then give you the distance and arrival time.

Additionally, I've included links in the "Resources" section of this book to other great circle calculators you can access on the Internet. Although some of these need conversion from kilometers or miles to nautical miles, they are a great backup to have, just in case.

Using the WaveCast® great circle online calculator to determine the distance from our storm's fetch (35N, 50W) to our forecast location (27N, 80W) we find this is a distance of 1609 nautical miles. The period of this swell is 12 seconds. We then have:

1609/(12 * 1.5) = 89.4 hours (**3.7 days**)

To finish this off we need to add in the time from the model as mentioned in Chapter 2. This model shows us that it is a 36 hour (1.5 days) projection (36h) from September 28th (20030928). This model was also initialized at 12Z, which for the forecast area of Florida, would work out to be 8:00 AM. Therefore, the actual forecast time for this swell works out to be:

3.7 days + 1.5 day projection = 5.2 days
Sep 28 8:00 AM + 5.2 days = **Oct 3 about 1:00 PM**

Using long-range models however, it's important to note that the calculations we performed are an estimate of the swell arrival and needs further monitoring. Many things can happen to a swell on its way to your beach, which we'll discuss more in Chapter 8, "Mitigating Factors". As such, your accuracy falls into what I like to call a funnel curve, illustrated in Figure 22.

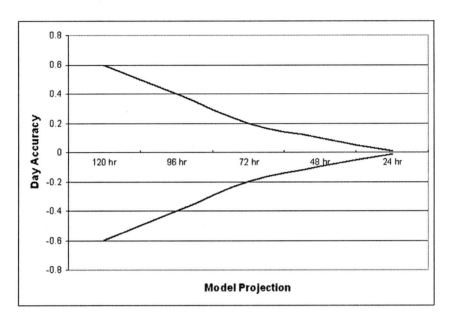

Figure 22 Funnel Curve of Accuracy

This is a rudimentary example of what you can expect, in a worse case scenario, from forecast accuracy using long-range models. The further out the model is forecasting, the looser the accuracy will be. For instance if you forecast a swell using a 120-hour model, you can expect—worse case—plus or minus 0.6 days (about 14 hours) of accuracy. A 72-hour model could give you an inaccuracy of plus or minus 0.2 days (about 5 hours).

Since we were using a 36 hour model, we can assume a tighter tolerance, shown on the funnel curve to be about plus or minus 0.1 days (about 2 ½ hours). Thus, our forecast for Oct. 3 at 1:00 PM could arrive within 2 ½ hours (either 10:30 AM or 3:30 PM). This is a confident forecast—only a couple hours either way.

Models with shorter-range projections (i.e. 0h-36h) will yield higher accuracy forecasts. This holds true not just for timing, but for size as well. As you get used to forecasting and logging swells, you'll get a better feel for how this tolerance works for your location, and the models you're using.

In any case, the arrival time calculations are easy, provided you could calculate the distance between the two coordinates (fetch and forecast location). Using the online calculator at WaveCast®, it wasn't too difficult. If you had to do this by hand however, you'd have to go through some pains, some of which is shown below[1]:

c = sin(phi1)*sin(phi2)*cos(theta1 - theta2) + cos(phi1)*cos(phi2)
distance = R*Arccos(c)*Pi/180

I get a headache just looking at that. Still, using this method is the most accurate. Using our online distance calculator, or others listed in the "Resources" chapter of this book, it can be less painful.

If you don't want to rely on the online distance calculator for every swell you are tracking, you could take a shortcut. This involves drawing out some great circle distance arcs on a model that you are used to using. This takes a little prep time, but you can produce some charts that show the approximations for swell arrival for a particular area. To show how this is done, I drew two great circle examples in Figures 23 and 24, using models from the Marine Modeling and Analysis Branch of NOAA.

---

1.   Dr. Math has a great explanation on this at http://mathforum.org/library/drmath/view/54680.html

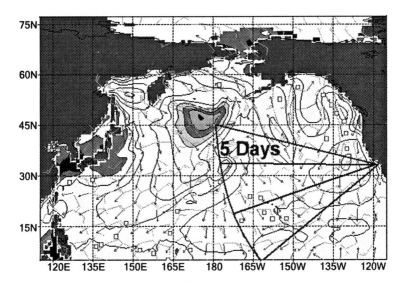

Figure 23 Great Circle Example for Southern California

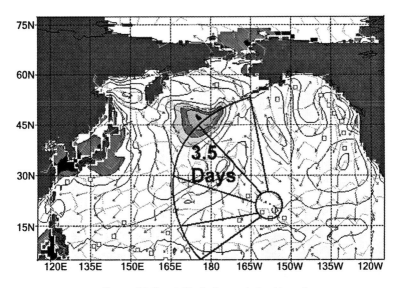

Figure 24 Great Circle Example for Hawaii

Each of these examples shows a great circle arc representing distance for swell arrival time. Once a storm's fetch hits the boundary depicted by the arc, swell is (approximately) that far away from hitting the forecast location. In the Hawaii example, a fetch that meets this arc will be about 3.5 days away from hitting

Hawaii. On the Southern California example, a fetch that meets the arc drawn on that model would be five days away from hitting Southern California.

For instance, notice there is a fetch with a leading edge near 45N, 180. On the Southern California model (Figure 23) the fetch is just touching the boundary of the great circle arc. This means that swell is 5 days away from hitting Southern California. The same fetch has already crossed the 3.5 day boundary in the Hawaii example in Figure 24, meaning the swell is less than 3.5 days away (probably about 3 or 3.2 days away).

Drawing multiple arcs on a model, you can see various times that swells could hit. You could draw 1-day, 2-day, 3-day, 4-day arcs or more, and keep this chart handy for quick reference. Drawing these charts can be a bit tedious, but once you have them, you can use them over and over again.

To make these great circle arc examples I used the online calculator (at http://wavecast.com/guide). I used an average ground swell period of 16 seconds for all the calculations. Then, I selected a time period for the distance. In the California example, I chose five days, and in the Hawaii example, I chose 3.5 days.

I kept the forecast location constant for each of these charts: 34N, 118W for California, and 22N, 158W for Hawaii. Then I merely picked out some possible fetch coordinates away from the forecast location, and drew an arc across these points. Getting those points however required some work. A quick way to get these points is to keep tweaking the fetch location coordinates in the great circle calculator until it gives you the time period you're aiming for. In the case of these examples, I was aiming for 5 days for CA, and 3.5 days for Hawaii.

For instance, in the California example, one of the fetch location coordinates I picked out was originally 30N, 180W. If you plugged this into the online calculator, you would have:

- Forecast Location: 34N 118W
- Fetch Location: 30N 180W
- **Result = 5.4 days**

Since I wanted a 5-day distance, I went back and tweaked the "Fetch Location" coordinates until I got five days. The coordinates turned out to be 31N, 176W. Then I drew a line from my forecast location (34N, 118W) to this location (31N, 176W). I continued this process of picking out fetch location coordinates, tweaking them until I got 5 days, and then drawing a line to them. Afterwards, I drew an arc across the end points of those lines. Notice that the arc may look distorted due to the Mercator projection. Nevertheless, if you are using drawing software, you could select a Bezier curve to connect the end points of your lines.

You can do the same for your forecast area, then keep these great circle charts close by to quickly reference approximations of swell arrival time. Bear in mind that I calculated the distances in these examples based on a 16-second period. This can vary, and needs accounted for. You could estimate that 18 and 20-second period swells will travel a tad faster, and that 12 and 14-second period swells will travel a bit slower.

Also, note that the lines I drew from the forecast location to each of the fetch coordinates were merely to get end points for drawing the great circle arc. The lines themselves have no other purpose. You could have just used plot points instead. I found it easier to see where I was by drawing by using straight lines.

For now, we'll continue with our other two examples using exact measurements from the WaveCast® online great circle calculator at http://wavecast.com/guide .

Let's look at our next example swell maker for a different forecast region in Figure 25.

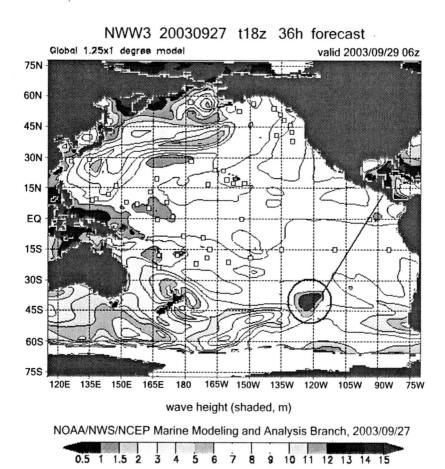

Figure 25 Southern Hemi Swell for Costa Rica

In this example, our storm fetch and location stats are:

- Storm/fetch location 35S, 115W
- The forecast location is Costa Rica, located at about 10N, 85W.
- Swell periods are 16 seconds

We'll assume that the significant wave heights are adequate enough to produce swell, and that this fetch is pointing towards our forecast region.

Plugging our coordinates into the online great circle calculator at the Wave-Cast® web site, we find that this storm is located about 3194 nautical miles away from Costa Rica. The period of this swell is 16 seconds, so we then have:

3194/(16*1.5) = 133 hours (**5.5 days**)

Let's take this example one step further, and look at the swell arrival time for Southern California from this same storm in the Southern Hemisphere, shown in Figure 26.

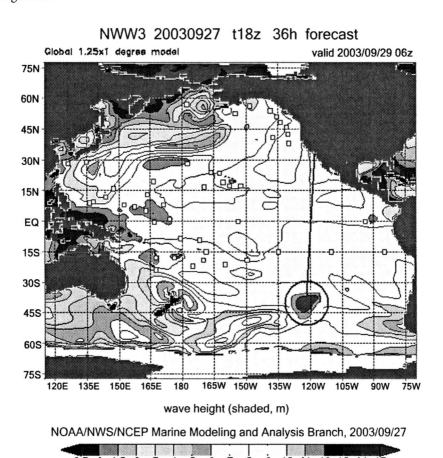

Figure 26 Southern Hemi Swell for Southern California

In this example, our location stats are a little different since the leading edge of the fetch relative to the forecast location is slightly different from our previous example. For our Southern California example in Figure 26 our stats are:

- Storm/fetch location 35S, 122W
- The forecast location is Southern California, located at about 34N, 118W.
- Periods are once again 16 seconds.

Using our online calculator, we find that the storm is located about 4149 nautical miles away from our forecast area. The period of this swell is 16 seconds, so we then have:

4149/(16*1.5) = 172.9 hours (about **7.2 days**)

That's all there is to it. Thanks to simple physics, and information from wave analysis models, we can calculate the timing of swell arrival. As I mentioned earlier, you can also perform this using pressure maps and Appendix B. Since I have access to the Internet, I prefer the quicker method of using WAM's.

There are some mitigating factors however, that could hinder the calculations we derived in our examples. We'll cover those in Chapter 8. For now, let's see how big waves will be once they arrive.

7

Knowing How Big

"Blue, green, grey, white, or black; smooth, ruffled, or mountainous; that ocean is not silent."

—H.P. Lovecraft

We've seen how large storms can produce surf that we see days later at our favorite surf spot. However, the size that we'll see, in most cases, will be much less than the significant wave height in the originating fetch. If you'll recall from our discussion on wave origination, energy dissipates as it travels through the water and air, which will reduce our wave size when we finally get some surf. Also, if a break isn't angled directly at the incoming swell, it won't see the full impact of the energy. Additionally, once the waves are at our beaches, they will not all break the same, nor will they be the same size at every break.

This leaves us with three primary elements to calculate the final face heights of the waves you'll be riding:

1. Loss of energy as the swell travels to the coast

2. Loss of energy if you're not directly facing the swell

3. Face height once the wave is ready to break

Before stepping into the calculations, let's take a brief look at the science behind a breaking wave, and see how this affects different types of breaks, and the amount of swell energy heading to the coast. We'll dig deeper into this subject in the next chapter. But for now, let's cover the basics to see the primary elements we need for calculating wave size.

Wave energy is just that: energy. Large storms in the ocean are not sending water to our coasts. Instead, wind energy driving the swell is transferred into the water. As this energy leaves the fetch, it dissipates, losing a lot of its strength on its way to the coast. As this energy travels through the ocean, it does so not only at the surface of the water, but also at a depth that is proportional to the amount of swell energy—the stronger the energy, the greater the depth. In deep water, this energy is far from the ocean floor. However, once this energy gets into shallower water, like the coastline, the energy hits the bottom and bounces back, forcing the water upwards. This makes the initial bulge on the horizon that makes you turn around and get ready to paddle.

As these initial waves approach the shore, the energy in them gets bunched up. The energy in front of the wave is slowing down due to friction with the shallow bottom. But, the energy behind the wave is still in deeper water, and is moving ahead at full speed. This energy behind the wave has no place to go but upwards, climbing the back of the bulging wave. This makes the top of the wave gain more speed, which forces the top of the wave to finally fall over and break. This is illustrated in Figure 27.

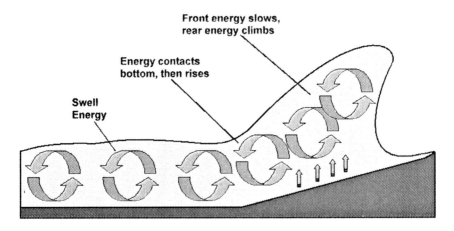

Figure 27 Swell Energy Turns into a Wave

The depth of the water and amount of swell energy coming in will determine the size of the waves. However, most coastlines are scattered with various types of breaks, each with a varying slope. Reefs tend to have a longer slope, allowing the incoming waves to rise more slowly, and not as big. Of course, this also means that the wave could break slower, and longer. Beach breaks tend to have a steeper slope, which makes the energy jump up more quickly. This tends to make the wave size bigger, but also tends to make for shorter rides.

We'll delve deeper into the physics of breaking waves when we discuss shoaling and refraction in the next chapter. For now, we know enough to start working on the three elements to calculate the wave size.

To gauge our first element—loss of energy as the swell travels to the coast—we use a "wave decay factor". As the swell energy makes its way to the coast, it doesn't loose its energy in an equal, linear fashion. Instead, the first leg of the journey will cause the swell to loose a lot of steam. Then, as the energy continues to travel, it slowly tapers off. Because of this non-linear energy loss, we can't use one single variable in our calculation. Nevertheless, the calculation for wave height after decay is simple:

Wave Height = (Swell Height) * (Wave Decay Factor)

But as mentioned, we first need to determine the wave decay factor. Assuming the fetch was created in deep water—as most swells are—allowing the swell energy to travel without interference with the ocean floor, we can obtain an average wave decay factor from the graph in Figure 28.

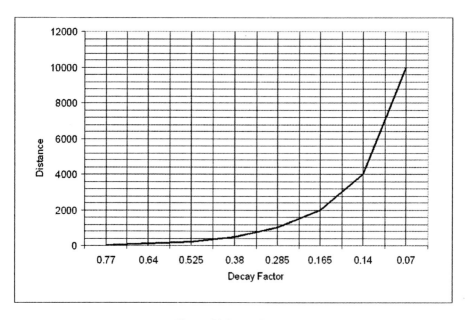

Figure 28 Decay Factor

This graph is based on energy loss through water over distance, showing estimates we can use for calculating expected wave size upon arrival to our forecast location. To see how this works, let's revisit our Florida example swell from Chapter 6. If you recall from this previous example, the swell heights were running 18 feet, and the storm was at a distance of 1609 nautical miles. Looking at the decay factor graph, we can see we would use the roughly estimated decay factor of 0.285

Let's plug these numbers into our wave height formula to see how this works out:

Wave Height = 18 * 0.285
Wave Height = **5.1 feet**

Thus, the 18-foot waves in the originating fetch decayed to 5.1 feet after traveling 1609 nautical miles.

Some areas have greater than normal decay, which needs to be taken into account. Storms forming in the Tasman Sea—located between Australia and

New Zealand—can be ideal for the local breaks on the east coast of Australia. However, swell-making systems moving north through this region will encounter an acute decay factor for other regions like California and Hawaii. Storms forming in the Tasman Sea face shallower ocean depths farther north and to the east, due to the numerous South Pacific islands. These islands, including New Caledonia, Vanuatu, Fiji, and Samoa have water depths around them ranging from only 200 to 2000 meters, compared with deeper water depths of 4000 meters or more in the lower portion of the Tasman Sea. These islands will soak up much of the energy before it can travel to California and Hawaii, causing greater than normal decay.

Knowing certain regions will cause greater than normal decay, you may need to tweak the numbers in the graph in Figure 28 for swells passing through those areas.

Energy loss is attributed to other factors as well, which brings us to our second element to calculate wave height: loss of energy depending on the angle of the swell to the forecast location. This is known as "angular spreading", and is discussed in more detail in the next chapter.

Angular spreading is a factor of energy dissipation based on forecast location and swell direction. In our last calculation, if we were directly facing the incoming swell, we would see a wave size of 5.1 feet. However, if we were angled away from the direction of the swell, we would see less. The percentage of loss is a non-linear function, but here are some estimates, based on your angle from the direction that the swell is heading:

- 90 degrees: at least 50–70% loss

- 75 degrees: about 30–50% loss

- 60 degrees: about 15–30% loss

- 45 degrees: about 10–15% loss

- 30 degrees: about 5–10% loss

- 15 degrees: about 5% loss

To calculate loss from angular spreading, we use this formula:

Wave Height = Wave Height - Angular Spreading

In our Florida example in Chapter 6, we assumed the swell was heading directly for Florida, so it would have no loss from angular spreading. But let's assume that the forecast location was angled at 15 degrees from the direction that the swell was heading. If this were the case, we would have a 5% loss of energy from angular spreading. Applying this to the 5.1-foot wave height after wave decay, we would have:

Wave Height = 5.1–5%
Wave Height = **4.8 feet**

We'll cover another example of angular spreading in Chapter 11, when we work out calculations for a hurricane that traveled at a steep angle away from its forecast location.

Now that we know how big the swell waves will be when they arrive, we can then calculate the last element: face height. If you'll recall from Chapter 1, the face height will be somewhat greater due to mitigating factors known as shoaling and refraction. Both of these factors have a lot to do with the period of the waves, the swell wave height, and the slope of the ocean floor, which we'll discuss in more detail in Chapter 8. Nevertheless, for now, as a rough estimate for face height, you can use what we call a "shoaling factor" using this formula:

Face Height = Wave Height * Shoaling Factor

Shoaling factors, which are based on the swell period are[1]:

- 20 seconds: 1.9

- 18 seconds: 1.85

- 16 seconds : 1.8

- 14 seconds: 1.6

---

1.   The shoaling factors are merely derived from our experience in calling swells. Many variables can affect shoaling, but are beyond the scope of our context here.

- 12 seconds: 1.3
- 10 seconds: 1.2
- 8 seconds: 1.1

In our Florida example in the previous chapter, we had a swell period of 12 seconds. After a decay of 1609 nautical miles (0.285 decay factor), we had a wave height of 5.1 feet (originally 18 feet in the fetch). Then if we subtract a loss of 5% from the angular spread of 15 degrees, we have a wave height of 4.8 feet. Using the shoaling calculation above, we would then calculate face height using a 1.3 shoaling factor for our 12-second period swell as follows:

Face Height = 4.8 * 1.3
Face Height = 6.2 feet (max)

Now let's put it all together. The actual face height of the waves you are forecasting would be calculated as follows:

Wave Height = (Swell Height) * (Wave Decay Factor)
Wave Height = Wave Height - Angular Spreading
Face Height = Wave Height * Shoaling factor

As we'll discuss more in the next chapter, there are other things to consider when factoring in shoaling (and refraction) for wave face height.

Now that we've covered the basics of knowing when, and how big, let's look at those mitigating factors affecting the surf you're predicting.

8

Mitigating Factors

One need only think of the weather, in which case the prediction even for a few days ahead is impossible.

—Albert Einstein

Mother Nature can be quite complex at times, especially when it comes to surf forecasting. We can look at storms forming over the deep waters of our oceans, and estimate to a certain degree the arrival time and size of the waves we'll receive. However, without taking into consideration mitigating factors, our forecast would be a best case (or worse case) scenario of what could occur.

Some of the things we need to take into account when making a surf prediction include:

- Shoaling
- Refraction
- Swell angles
- Swell windows and angular spreading
- Diffraction
- Island blockage (also referred to as shadowing)
- Opposing winds and currents
- Storm course

Let's look at these mitigating factors and see how they affect surf forecast predictions.

Shoaling

Shoaling is the most important factor when calculating the face height of waves. This factor depends on two things:

- The length of the periods
- The slope of the ocean floor in the surf zone

Both elements can come together to make face height different from one surf spot to another, even during the same swell. But in other swells, almost all surf spots could have the same face height. Knowing how these elements work together will help you to refine your forecasts so you will know how big the wave faces will be at your favorite surf spots depending on the type of swell coming in.

Shoaling is what occurs when a wave approaches shallow water. This is shown somewhat in Figure 27 in Chapter 7. In deep water, where waves form and travel to the coast, the wave energy is far away from the ocean floor, and travels along uninterrupted. As waves enter shallower water however, wave energy makes contact with the ocean floor, which forces the water to rise up and eventually break.

The energy of a wave is directly proportional to its period. Long period waves, like those in a ground swell, have more energy than short period waves comprising a wind swell. Long period waves start to interact with the ocean floor well before short period waves. In fact, the energy in a wave will begin to touch bottom at a depth equal to ½ its wavelength. Therefore, the longer the period of the swell, the sooner waves will begin to shoal. Once a wave begins to shoal, its energy has to rise since it is being forced off the ocean floor. Thus, a 4-foot wave with a 16-second period, like that in a ground swell, will start to shoal well before a 4-foot wave with only a 10-second period.

The sooner a wave begins to shoal, the bigger the face height. Since longer period waves shoal earlier, they grow more intensely, break sooner, and have bigger faces. Hence, a 4-foot ground swell wave (i.e. 16 second periods) will turn into a bigger wave in the surf zone than a 4-foot wind swell wave (i.e. 10 second periods).

A property of wave physics known as "wave steepness" controls the effect of shoaling based on the wavelength of the incoming waves. Wavelength and the wave period are closely related—they both have to do with the space between waves. Period is the time between the waves—wavelength is the distance. Wave steepness is a ratio of the wave height to the wavelength:

Steepness = Wave Height/Wavelength

When this ratio exceeds 1/7, the wave becomes unstable and begins to break. Shorter period waves have a shorter wavelength, so their steepness ratio exceeds the 1/7 limit more rapidly than longer period waves. For instance, a wave approaching the coast with a wavelength of 7 meters (21 feet) would begin to break once the wave reached a height (i.e. from shoaling) of 1 meter (3 feet).

1 meter/7 meters = 1/7 max steepness (wave breaks)

But if the wavelength were shorter, say by half as much (3.5 meters) then the wave would reach the steepness ratio at only 0.5 meters.

0.5 meter/3.5 meters = 1/7 max steepness (wave breaks)

Hence, longer period waves can build into bigger waves as they shoal, resulting in bigger face heights[1].

When the wave reaches maximum steepness and is ready to break, it does so in water that is usually 1.3 times the wave height (as it builds from shoaling). If the slope of the ocean floor near a surf spot has an abrupt slope, this change in water depth is sudden, which can result in an increase in wave size as well. Long period waves have more energy than short period waves, so long period waves travel faster. Faster waves will shoot up more quickly in relation to the slope angle. This means that as long period waves shoal, they have bigger wave faces at spots with an abrupt slope on the ocean floor. If your surf spot has a gradual slope, then waves will break slower and can be smaller.

---

1.   Technically speaking, the wavelength will shorten a bit as the wave begins to shoal, but the period remains the same, which increases wave height as well. But for simplicity of this discussion, wavelength and wave period are practically synonymous.

Taking into account the period of the swell, and the slope of the ocean floor at particular breaks, you can predict varying face heights from one place to another. For instance, when a long-period ground swell hits the coast, the kiddy beach, bunny slope, old man longboard break probably has a slow-sloped floor, making the waves slow rolling, and moderately sized. During this same long-period ground swell, the short board break—with a steeper and quicker slope on the ocean floor—would probably have some fast-spitting barrels with wave faces almost twice as high as the bunny slope break.

On a short period wind swell however, both surf spots would have wave faces nearly equal in size. Remember that the actual wave face height will depend on the steepness of the wave *and* the steepness of the ocean floor. The one variable that can change this from swell to swell is the wave period.

As such, shoaling is a more noticeable factor when there are long-period ground swells, resulting in bigger wave faces at faster beach break spots, and smaller wave faces at the slower reef breaks[2]. When there are short-period wind swells on the other hand, the two surf spots come closer together in size.

As mentioned in Chapter 7, we can use the following formula to calculate wave face height from shoaling:

Face Height = Wave Height * Shoaling Factor

Roughly estimated, shoaling factors for swell period are[3]:

- 20 seconds: 1.9
- 18 seconds: 1.85
- 16 seconds : 1.8
- 14 seconds: 1.6
- 12 seconds: 1.3

2.   The type of break—beach or reef—is a generalization. Many reefs can be just as steep as beach breaks. The variable to be aware of is slope angle of the ocean floor at the break.

3.   I'd like to reiterate that these shoaling factors are merely derived from experience, and many other variables beyond the scope of this context need consideration.

- 10 seconds: 1.2
- 8 seconds: 1.1

As we can see, the shorter the period of the swell, the less effect shoaling will make on differentiating size between disparate surf spots. However, without knowing the slope of the ocean floor and other characteristics of the surf spot you're forecasting, it would be very difficult to obtain an exact face height measurement from shoaling.

Although the above numbers work in many cases, it's important that you get to know how your favorite surf spots will work an incoming swell. For instance, you might find these factors work well for the beach breaks at your area, but need to be toned down a bit for the slower reefs. Figure 29 illustrates such an example:

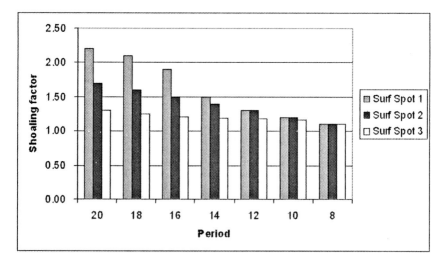

Figure 29 Example Shoaling Factors

As this chart shows, you might have three different surf spots to predict the face height resulting from shoaling. Surf spot 1 is a fast beach break that typically gets bigger and faster waves. Surf spot 2 is a more moderate break, and spot 3 is a very slow rolling break. Notice how the shoaling factor for all three breaks drops off and becomes about equal when we are in short period surf like a wind swell, but has a more dramatic difference in longer period surf.

In any case, remember that the period of the wave has a dramatic effect on face height. Longer periods from a ground swell can result in larger face heights than the shorter periods of a wind swell. Another factor can affect face-height however: refraction, which is the topic of our next mitigating factor.

Refraction

Refraction and shoaling work hand in hand. Refraction is a process of waves bending as they shoal, which can cause various effects. In short, refraction is a factor that like shoaling, can affect the size of waves as they prepare to break.

When waves arrive from a direction that is perpendicular to a straight beach, the wave crests will parallel the beach. However, if the waves come in from an angle, or the beach is not perfectly straight (which is common), the waves will bend, trying to conform to the contours of the ocean floor and coastline. This refraction will cause a change in both height and direction in shallow water near the beach.

Refraction can increase the size and strength of a breaking wave. When a wave is heading towards a beach from an angle, one portion of the wave will start to shoal (make contact with the bottom) before the rest of the wave. This will slow the initial portion of the wave, but the remainder of the wave moves ahead at full speed, wheeling around the slower portion. Eventually, provided the strength of the wave is great enough, the wave will swing completely around, making the entire wave head straight for the beach with one massive force.

Additionally, refraction can cause size to increase at reefs and points where the incoming wave energy focuses on the point. Such is the case with the infamous Jaws off the coast of Maui, known for its enormous 70-foot waves[4]. When waves approach a ridge, (or point), the portion of the wave crest over the ridge slows down more than the wave crests on either side, which allows the wave to focus its energy more directly on the point. This concentration of energy results in bigger waves at the point.

Refraction differs from one spot to another from differences on the ocean floor, often referred to as bathymetry (depth measurements). If a long-period

---

4.   A great refraction study for Jaws is online at http://www.coastal.udel.edu/ngs/

wave encounters the right bathymetry, it can cause larger waves for some breaks compared to others during the same swell. Underwater canyons and sand bars are good examples of this as they cause various differences in the water depths along the coastline.

Like shoaling, refraction is more noticeable with long period swells, and is less noticeable with shorter period swells, as this factor is proportional to the wave energy (e.g. the period). And like shoaling, you will notice differences between sizes in short period wind swells compared to long period ground swells. However, the difference with refraction compared to shoaling, is that refraction is mainly affected by the angle of the incoming swell.

Refraction is a difficult factor to calculate, and requires information regarding the ocean floor topography. As such, it's recommended that for simple surf forecasting, you merely maintain awareness of this factor, and get to know how your surf spots react from various types of swells, and their angles.

Since refraction relates to shoaling, but is dependent on the angle of the incoming swell, you can tweak your shoaling factors for breaks that you notice take on more refraction, and increase in size more than others do. Breaks that pull in the bigger waves as a result of shoaling and refraction are often referred to as "standout spots" in our WaveCast® reports.

Alternatively, instead of using a single shoaling variable, you could make tables of modified shoaling factors for each of your favorite surf spots based on how they work from shoaling (period) and refraction (angle) as shown below

Surf Spot A

Period	270 Deg.	300 Deg.	310 Deg.
20	2.80	1.90	1.30
18	2.70	1.70	1.25
16	2.50	1.50	1.21
14	1.80	1.40	1.19
12	1.60	1.30	1.18

Period	270 Deg.	300 Deg.	310 Deg.
10	1.30	1.20	1.16
8	1.10	1.10	1.10

This table is an example of shoaling factors based on angles of refraction for one surf spot, and you could make tables for other surf spots as well.

Surf Spot B

Period	270 Deg.	300 Deg.	310 Deg.
20	2.10	1.80	1.30
18	2.00	1.50	1.25
16	1.90	1.40	1.21
14	1.70	1.30	1.19
12	1.60	1.20	1.18
10	1.30	1.10	1.16
8	1.10	1.10	1.10

Deriving the numbers for each surf spot could be arduous, requiring observations from numerous swells at your favorite breaks. Nevertheless, after monitoring for some time you'll realize that your area typically has only a few primary swell directions, making the task of gathering data less painful.

Swell Angles

Along with the type of break, and its slope, we also have to consider the angle the beach is facing. Figure 30 shows a portion of the Northern California coastline to illustrate how angles affect the incoming swell.

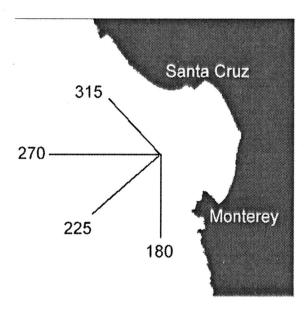

Figure 30 Angles for Incoming Swell

Although this diagram shows only a small view of the coast, we can see that the area around Santa Cruz faces more southerly, Monterey faces more westerly, and in some places, northwest. If a swell were coming in from 225 degrees, it would fill into areas that have some exposure to the south, like Santa Cruz. Monterey on the other hand, may not see as much of this energy. Instead, a west facing area like Monterey would pick up a swell with a more westerly angle like 270, or perhaps 315.

The swell angle is a major factor when calculating wave size, and is a portion of the next mitigating factor regarding swell windows and angular spread. To use these next factors well, it's advisable to know the direction that your favorite breaks face, and realize what swell angles will work them best.

Swell Windows and Angular Spreading

Swell windows and angular spreading are factors when estimating size. As waves leave the fetch from the originating storm, they tend to fan out, similar to the "pebble in the pond" analogy we discussed in Chapter 4. If your break is in a direct path of an incoming swell, then it will get the most impact. However, if your break is angled at 15 degrees from the path of the swell, then you can expect less energy, and smaller waves. If you were angled at 45 degrees away, then you would see even less of the energy.

There's some intense math to calculate what is known as the "angular spread" of the swell, and how much of it will hit your area. To simplify this, first you have to determine if your break is even in a swell window for this energy. In other words, is there anything blocking the swell from coming in? For instance in Figure 30, a 190-degree swell would more than likely completely miss the northern part of Monterey (the cut out above the M in Monterey). This would be completely out of the swell window. Santa Cruz on the other hand would be partially in the swell window.

If your surf spot falls within a swell window, you can use some angular spread estimates like those used in Chapter 7. These are:

- 90 degrees: at least 50–70% loss

- 75 degrees: about 30–50% loss

- 60 degrees: about 15–30% loss

- 45 degrees: about 10–15% loss

- 30 degrees: about 5–10% loss

- 15 degrees: about 5% loss

It is important to note that the angle you perceive on the Mercator (flat) models could be different from a great circle measurement, which is the more accurate. The longer away the fetch is that you're measuring, the higher likelihood of some distortion in the angle. However, when it comes to angular spreading, this tends to be negligible for the estimates shown above.

Diffraction

Diffraction is a change in direction and intensity of waves after passing by an obstacle. This occurs quite often at south facing breaks that pull in what we often call "wrap action" from west or northwest swells. Although the swell energy may be coming in from the west or northwest, if the shoreline curves around (like many areas in California) the energy diffracts, and bends toward the hidden portion of the coastline.

Diffraction can be a good thing as it can bring surf to beaches not directly facing the angle of the incoming swell. Diffracted waves are weaker as well, which can help to filter the energy. For instance, a big northwest swell hitting the California coast would pound the west facing areas, but south facing breaks, like the Santa Cruz region shown in Figure 30, would be cleaner yet smaller from diffracted energy that wrapped in.

Diffraction can be a hard thing to calculate upfront. As with shoaling and refraction, diffraction is one of those factors you can estimate with experience, observing how swells from various angles affect all the breaks, not just the ones facing the swell.

Island Blockage

Island blockage occurs when an island stands in the way of incoming swell energy, acting as a barrier. This is illustrated in Figure 31.

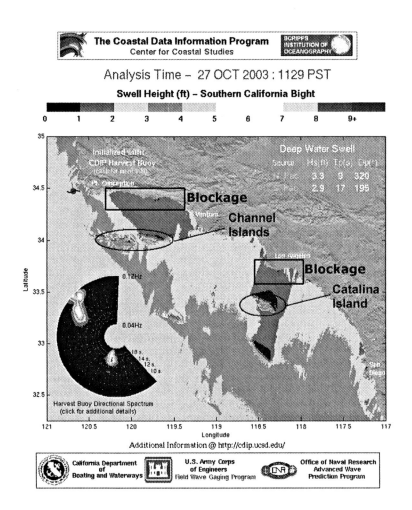

Figure 31 Example of Island Blockage

This model, provided by the Coastal Data Information Program (CDIP) shows how island blockage affects certain areas of Southern California. In this model, we can see a south swell is blocked by Catalina Island, causing a shadowing effect on certain portions of Los Angeles and northern Orange County. Similar effects can be seen east of Pt. Conception in Santa Barbara, shadowed by the Channel Islands from the south swell.

If you surf in an area that has islands off the coast, like Southern California, be aware of these island obstacles, and get to know the swell angles that they affect.

If you have access to swell models like those provided by the CDIP for California, you can visualize the island blockage effect for various swell angles. If you don't have access to swell models, then you might use a protractor to draw various angles on a map of your forecast area; thereby, seeing what angles could affect the region.

Opposing Winds and Currents

Winds and seas that oppose incoming swells may have some slightly negative effects. Let's revisit that ground swell for Florida that we were tracking in Chapter 6. Figure 32 shows a close up view near the coast of Florida from the period model.

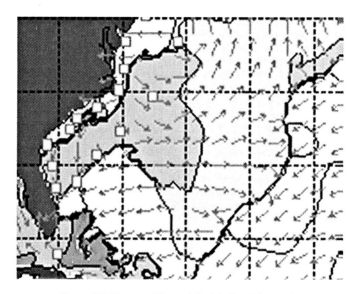

Figure 32 Close-up View of Florida Swell Example

Notice how there appears to be opposing currents in this model that seem to be "pushing" against the incoming swell from the ENE. This has some influence, but the model is somewhat deceiving.

A well known oceanographer, Walter Munk, conducted a study in 1963 where he was able to prove that waves traveling across large bodies of water, like the Pacific, have little dampening in wave energy due to opposing swells. Munk tracked waves that developed in storms near Antarctica, crossed the equator and eventually reached the shores of Alaska. His study showed that there was negligible loss in wave energy after factoring in the expected decay.

Still, there are five main reasons for wave dissipation:

1. Internal friction within the waves.

2. Resistance met as waves overtake the wind.

3. Restraint caused by crosswinds.

4. Action of ocean currents in the path of waves.

5. Effects of seaweed, ice, shoals, islands, or continents in the path of waves.

Even with all these factors working to bring about wave dissipation, swell waves dissipate very gradually. In fact, opposing winds have approximately a 10 times weaker impact on dissipation than the energy of the wave itself. However, if currents crossing a swell's path are strong enough, they could change the direction of the swell. This is more likely to happen, but it takes a lot of current to do this. In essence, the swell energy is still high, no matter what. Nevertheless, the swell might change course on its way to the coast if strong enough currents or winds cross its path. Also, if opposing winds are strong enough, they could dampen the swell, although it is more likely that these strong winds would have an impact on the current.

No matter how you slice it, keep an eye out for strong opposing winds and currents, and get to know how they affect your surf spots. Wind and currents follow patterns. Knowing these patterns will help you spot a potential dampening effect.

In the Pacific, there is a change in currents from the summer to winter seasons. This will favor Northern Hemisphere swells in the winter, and Southern Hemisphere swells in the summer. Albeit, these are the times when those hemispheres produce storms; thus, making it more likely for those swell patterns, and currents to flow.

If there were a strong enough current to inhibit swell energy, it would probably shift the course of the storm anyways. For instance, in the case of the Pacific, let's say you saw a storm form near New Zealand. If this were summer in the US (winter down under), you'd probably see the storm move north, favoring the seasonal currents, and pushing some south swell to California beaches. But during the fall or winter, you may see that storm move directly east, following the seasonal currents and wind patterns. Remember that angular spreading (discussed in Chapter 7) tells us that the greater the angle we are away from the direction of the incoming swell, the weaker the resultant surf will be. Therefore, with the storm moving easterly, instead of northerly, the angle of the storm's direction to California would be more along the lines of 90 degrees, which, as discussed in Chapter 7 would be a loss of energy well over 50%.

Storm Course

Not all storms follow a straight path. Quite often you'll find a storm will travel towards a coastline, then be diverted above or below the expected trajectory. Looking at long-range models you can see the expected course for a storm system. But of course, you will need to keep a close watch on the storm each day to see what it will do. If we look back at our Florida swell example again, this storm over a course of a couple days took a diverted path shown in Figure 33.

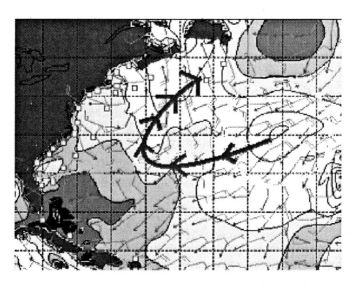

Figure 33 Actual Diverted Path of Florida Swell Example

Many times a particular area, and its seasons, will have repeated patterns for storm trajectory. Getting to know these for your particular area will help you to place a confidence level on your forecasts knowing the potential for a storm's diversion.

Storms that divert away from a coast tend to give what we call "reflective" energy[5] in our WaveCast® reports. The swell from a reflected system can still be calculated with a fair amount of accuracy. Just take the measurement around the time of the diversion. Once it angles away, then you're up against swell loss from the angular spread.

---

5.   The term "reflective energy" is a slang term used in our forecast reports, and is not meant as a scientific definition. Reflection in wave analysis has a different meaning.

9

Tides

o o o o o o o o o o o o o o o o o o o o o o o o o o o o o o o o o

The tide rises, the tide falls,
The twilight darkens, the curlew calls;
The little waves, with their soft, white hands,
Efface the footprints in the sands,
And the tide rises, the tide falls.

—Henry Wadsworth Longfellow

Tides play an important role in planning your sessions. Every day, usually twice a day, the tides come in, and back out again. Each day the times and height of the low and high tides will vary. This means that constantly, due to tides, the water depth at your favorite surf spot will differ. Depending on the break, it may work better with a lower tide due to the decreased depth of the water. On the other hand, if the tide is too high, then the water may be too deep for an incoming swell to break.

Knowing how tides are made can shed some light on how to utilize tide times to your advantage, making them a vital piece of any surf forecast. The great thing about tide information is that it can be predicted. This is the only condition in the whole gambit of surf data that you can predict with near 100% accuracy, every time.

Getting tide information is easy. There are tons of tide tables you can buy and access online, including free daily tide tables at the WaveCast® reports on wet-sand.com.

Tide heights are relative to sea level. For instance, a high tide of 4 feet means that the tide for that time will be 4 feet above sea level. A low tide of -2 feet means that the tide will be two feet below the normal sea level.

Below is an example tide entry for a 24-hour period for Santa Monica, California:

2003–09–29	6:52 PM PDT	0.10 feet	Low Tide
2003–09–30	1:10 AM PDT	3.87 feet	High Tide
2003–09–30	6:02 AM PDT	2.18 feet	Low Tide
2003–09–30	12:34 PM PDT	5.93 feet	High Tide

This shows how the tide typically rises high twice a day, and dips to a low twice a day as well.

But what are these tides, and how will they affect your sessions? The Earth alone does not cause tides. Instead, the Moon is the greatest factor.

Gravity keeps everything on our planet pulled toward its center. This not only includes our bodies, buildings, and other objects. It also includes the water in the ocean. All masses have a certain amount of gravitational pull. The larger the mass, the larger the gravity that it exerts on objects near it. For instance, the Sun is quite larger than the Earth, which influences a gravitational pull on the Earth to stay in its orbit around the Sun. The Earth is a larger mass than the Moon, influencing the Moon to stay close by due to the Earth's gravitational pull.

The strength of gravity is influenced by the closeness of objects. The closer an object is to a mass, the greater the gravitational effect on the object. Since the Earth is not evenly round, due to mountains, and other such protrusions, there are some slight variations in gravity all over our planet. Nevertheless, these effects rarely have any bearing on mountains and other solid objects. Water, on the other hand, is fluid and is pulled more easily.

The Moon is constantly pulling on the Earth ever so slightly, enough to pull the oceans closer to it. Since the mountains and other solid objects don't move from this gravitational pull from the Moon, we see the oceans pulled, then released depending on the orbits of both the Earth and the Moon. Each pull causes a high tide on one side of the Earth. But the water has to be taken from somewhere, the location of the corresponding low tide. This is illustrated in Figure 34.

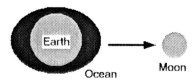

Figure 34 Tidal Pull from Moon

Besides the Moon, the Sun's gravity also influences the Earth's oceans as well. Since we have different seasons, the tides tend to differ in their variations from season to season. For instance, winter season in Southern California tends to have tides that often reach highs of 6 or 7 feet. However, during the summer, the fluctuation is typically only to highs in the 4-foot range.

Full Moons and New Moons affect the tide as well. These lunar events occur when the Sun, Earth, and Moon are directly in line with each other. This causes a greater gravitational pull on the Earth's oceans from two directions: one from the Sun, the other from the Moon. This creates greater fluctuations between high and low tide levels. It's as though the Sun and Moon are fighting to see who can pull the Earth's oceans the most.

Tide tables are very reliable means to determine the high and low tide times for practically any spot on the planet. During our lifetimes, the tide times will remain constant. However, there are some minor things happening to the gravitational pull, and Earth's rotation, that will affect tides in millions of years from now. For instance, the Earth and Moon rotate at different speeds, which contribute in part to the varying time for tides to occur. However, the constant tugging and pulling of the forces between the Earth and Moon will eventually cause these two heavenly bodies to rotate at the same period (at least in theory). Thus, in about a billion years or so, we may need to redo our tide tables. But for now, these minuscule variations are unnoticeable.

Until the Moon and Earth have equal orbital paths and rotation periods, tidal times and heights will fluctuate each day. Going back to our Santa Monica example earlier, let's look at a four-day period, and see how not only the times for the tides change, but also their heights.

Santa Monica, California

2003–09–30	1:10 AM PDT	3.87 feet	High Tide
2003–09–30	6:02 AM PDT	2.18 feet	Low Tide
2003–09–30	12:34 PM PDT	5.93 feet	High Tide
2003–09–30	8:07 PM PDT	0.24 feet	Low Tide
2003–10–01	2:50 AM PDT	3.42 feet	High Tide
2003–10–01	6:46 AM PDT	2.77 feet	Low Tide
2003–10–01	1:34 PM PDT	5.62 feet	High Tide
2003–10–01	9:36 PM PDT	0.29 feet	Low Tide
2003–10–02	5:10 AM PDT	3.46 feet	High Tide
2003–10–02	8:10 AM PDT	3.25 feet	Low Tide
2003–10–02	2:57 PM PDT	5.33 feet	High Tide
2003–10–02	11:06 PM PDT	0.16 feet	Low Tide
2003–10–03	6:38 AM PDT	3.86 feet	High Tide
2003–10–03	10:32 AM PDT	3.31 feet	Low Tide
2003–10–03	4:35 PM PDT	5.24 feet	High Tide

Tides are different from place to place, even from one city to the next along the coast. This is due to a number of factors, including the fact that the Earth and its ocean depths are not even, and the location of the Moon will be slightly different from location to location as well. For instance, let's look at a similar tide table for the same days as our last example, but from Santa Barbara, California, north of Santa Monica by about 60 miles.

Santa Barbara, California

2003–09–30	1:40 AM PDT	3.69 feet	High Tide
2003–09–30	6:23 AM PDT	2.24 feet	Low Tide
2003–09–30	12:56 PM PDT	5.81 feet	High Tide
2003–09–30	8:33 PM PDT	0.10 feet	Low Tide
2003–10–01	3:25 AM PDT	3.32 feet	High Tide
2003–10–01	7:09 AM PDT	2.80 feet	Low Tide
2003–10–01	1:56 PM PDT	5.54 feet	High Tide
2003–10–01	10:00 PM PDT	0.10 feet	Low Tide
2003–10–02	5:41 AM PDT	3.44 feet	High Tide
2003–10–02	8:36 AM PDT	3.24 feet	Low Tide
2003–10–02	3:18 PM PDT	5.28 feet	High Tide
2003–10–02	11:25 PM PDT	-0.03 feet	Low Tide
2003–10–03	6:59 AM PDT	3.81 feet	High Tide
2003–10–03	10:52 AM PDT	3.26 feet	Low Tide
2003–10–03	4:51 PM PDT	5.19 feet	High Tide

Notice how the times and heights vary between these two locales, spaced only 60 miles apart. No two places on the plant have the exact same gravitational pull at any one moment in time. Therefore, our tides will be different for the exact same time from place to place.

Although the tides will differ between your favorite surf spots, they don't vary as much within shorter distances. The greater the distance from your tide table readings, the greater the difference in tide times and heights. Tide tables for every exact location are hard to come by. Nevertheless, you can get a close enough approximation by finding a tide reading within 10 to 20 miles of your favorite surf spots.

As mentioned, tide levels can affect your session. If you surf during a 3-foot tide, you might notice in a few hours that the waves aren't breaking as well. The waves could be mushier, slower, and have less power. If this is the case, you might have been out long enough for the 3-foot tide to climb even higher, possibly to over 5 or 6 feet.

On the other hand, you might have noticed during your session that the waves were breaking a little farther out, and the waves were getting paper thin. Then eventually, the waves may not be breaking at all. In this case, you may have hit a negative tide, possibly a foot or more below sea level.

Although tides will vary in height between the low and high tide times, the amount of variance is important. In our WaveCast® reports, we call a massive fluctuation in tidal heights a "tidal swing". If the difference between the high and low tide times is greater than 5 feet, then this could have a noticeable impact on how the waves will work a particular break.

If you'll recall from Chapter 8 when we talked about shoaling, waves break depending on the depth of the water, typically when the incoming wave reaches a water depth that is 1.3 times the wave height. Therefore, a 4-foot wave will start to break in water that is 5.2 feet deep. Going back to our example session where you were surfing at a 3-foot tide, let's say that near the end of your session the tide rose to 6 feet. This increased the water depth by 3 feet. Therefore, waves that were breaking 100 feet away from shore now have to travel further toward the coast to meet shallower water. Where once there was 5.2 feet of water during the 3-foot tide, there is now 8.2 feet of water at the 6-foot tide.

Surfing is truly a sport that's dependant on many factors of nature. Tide times are most definitely one of those many factors. Although we can always predict time times and heights by using tide tables, it takes experience and observation to know how the tide levels will affect your favorite surf spots.

10

Seasonal Effects

Live in each season as it passes; breathe the air, drink the drink, taste the fruit, and resign yourself to the influences of each. Let them be your only diet drink and botanical medicines.

—*Henry David Thoreau*

If you've ever tuned in to the radio talk show "Let's Talk Surfing" with Marc Kent, you may have caught one of the quarterly interviews where Marc and I talk about the long-range projections for the upcoming seasons. About every three to four months, Marc and I chat about trends occurring across the oceans, and their influence on surf over the next few months. Even though there are typical trends to expect from season to season, Mother Nature throws many variables into the mix. Understanding these variables can shed some light on extreme long-range projections, as well as standard long-range forecasts.

Every season has a unique pattern for each region on the planet. The Northern Hemisphere winters bring snow to many of the northern states in the US. Summer on the other hand is a reverse of this pattern. Spring and autumn are seasons that transition between the two extremes. Similarly, the oceans react differently from season to season, and have transition periods as well.

Just as some winters may be colder than other winters, and some summers may be hotter than other summers, our oceans also encounter extreme conditions. One summer could see more swells than the year before, and the winter could see flatter surf then the prior year. These fluctuations are not all by chance. By looking at ocean trends, we can predict, to a certain degree, how an upcoming season may turn out in the way of surf.

A few primary contributors influence shifts in seasonal swell intensity, and frequency to occur. The most familiar of these are the El Niño and La Niña phenomena. In addition, there is the Pacific Decadal Oscillation (PDO) that can play a role as well. Nevertheless, these events only intensify or weaken the normal seasonal pattern. So let's first look at some typical seasonal trends, and then see how ocean phenomena like El Niño and La Niña affect these patterns.

Weather is driven by the power of the Sun. As solar energy, radiating from the Sun reaches Earth, regions closer to the Equator heat up more than the poles, located at the extremes of the planet. As land or ocean waters warm up, it heats the air next to it and this air begins to rise. As hot air rises, air from other places flows in to replace it. If you recall from the discussion on winds in Chapter 5, low-pressure systems, where the air is rising, pulls in air from around it.

If the Earth were not rotating on its axis, the air flowing in to replace the rising air would come from the polar regions. In this scenario, the air that rises near the Equator would be flowing high above the ground, to descend and replace the air that's flowing along the surface toward the tropics.

However, the Earth is rotating, which causes air to turn and swirl as it flows in to replace the rising air in a low-pressure system. Furthermore, the Earth is tilted. It's because of this tilt that we have seasons. During the Northern Hemisphere summer, the Earth tilts towards the Sun. Sunlight focuses on the Northern Hemisphere, which warms up the US and other regions north of the Equator. Conversely, during the Northern Hemisphere winter, the Earth tilts away from the Sun, resulting in the Northern Hemisphere soaking up much less sunlight. During spring and fall, the Earth's tilt allows the sun to focus on the Equator, equalizing the effects on both hemispheres.

Because of this tilt, the Northern Hemisphere is always angled in the opposite direction of the Southern Hemisphere. This reciprocates the seasons between the hemispheres. When we have a winter in the Northern Hemisphere, it's summer in the Southern Hemisphere. And when it's summer in the Northern Hemisphere, it's winter in the Southern Hemisphere.

Storms can develop all year round across the globe. However, there are two primary types of storm patterns, no matter what hemisphere you're looking at.

The two types of storm patterns correlate with the extreme seasons. There is a winter storm pattern, and a summer storm pattern. Spring and fall seasons are transition periods between these two. Getting to know seasonal weather patterns for your region increases the forecast accuracy by anticipating swell generation for various regions affecting your local surf spots.

During a winter pattern, storms tend to be quite active in the colder water regions. In the Northern Hemisphere for instance, Pacific storms tend to form during the winter with massive intensity kicking up swell heights 25 feet or greater, even at times towards 45 feet or more. The jet stream and ocean currents push these massive swells from the Western Pacific and Aleutian Chain region towards the west coast of the US. These systems throw the familiar northwest swells at Hawaii and California during the Northern Hemisphere winter months, making spots like Pipeline and Mavericks go off. These enormous storms trend the mean wave direction along their trajectory, resulting in a powerful force of dominant northwest current in the ocean waters in the Northern Hemisphere.

On the flip side, a summer in the Northern Hemisphere has much quieter activity. The mean wave direction is not as dominant from the northwest. Instead, it's wintertime in the Southern Hemisphere, and large systems are forming below the Equator, typically as far down as the ice cap, and New Zealand. These large storms are responsible for most of the southwest swells that hit the west coast of the US and Hawaii during the Northern Hemisphere summer. Even though it may be summer in the Northern Hemisphere, a winter pattern in the Southern Hemisphere can spawn the swell making systems that throw surf to breaks in the Northern Hemisphere.

The second primary storm pattern is the summer storm pattern. This is a combination of:

1. Tropical cyclones (hurricanes, typhoons, etc.), that form near your region.

2. Swell generated from a winter pattern in the hemisphere opposite of your region.

In Southern California for instance, our summer is mainly a mix of swells from Southern Hemisphere winter storms, and hurricanes that form north of the Equator.

So there are the two patterns. We have wintertime surf hitting us from a particular hemisphere, and rogue cyclone systems to account for in the summer. But as mentioned, there are forces of nature that influence these patterns to their extremes.

El Niño and La Niña—and to some degree the Pacific Decadal Oscillation (PDO)—will swing the extreme of the seasonal pattern one way or another. During an El Niño winter in 1997 to 1998, storms from the Pacific wreaked havoc on Hawaii and California coastlines. This event intensified the typical seasonal pattern of winter storms, making the storms larger, more powerful, and forcing them into a slightly different course.

So what exactly are El Niño, La Niña, and the PDO? The term El Niño was first used by Peruvian fishermen in the late 1800's to describe the warm current appearing off the western coast of Peru around Christmas time. El Niño is Spanish for "the child", but is often referred to as "the Christ child"; hence, its association with Christmas time.

Today El Niño describes an oscillation of sea surface temperatures in the tropical Pacific. This oscillation is associated with the atmosphere, and is often referred to as the ENSO (El Niño Southern Oscillation). La Niña also participates in the ENSO, and is the opposite of an El Niño.

During normal seasons—not affected by El Niño or La Niña—sea surface temperatures (SST's) are about 6–8 degrees Celsius warmer in the western tropical Pacific than they are in the eastern tropical Pacific. This normal difference in temperature is mainly due to the easterly trade winds that normally blow across the Pacific. These trade winds move the water on the surface from the eastern Pacific to the western Pacific along the equatorial region.

But during an El Niño event, trade winds either lighten up, or sometimes reverse their direction across the equatorial Pacific. This allows the warmer waters to build up where they shouldn't. During a La Niña, the easterly trade winds strengthen, which intensifies cold water upwelling, placing colder water where it shouldn't be. In both cases, this disturbs the normal balance of the Earth's weather, resulting in an upset in the seasonal storm patterns. Since the effects of

El Niño and La Niña are directly opposite, their effects on the weather, and consequently the storms that bring us swell, tend to be opposite as well.

The jet streams, during an El Niño or La El Niña event, are disrupted by not only intensity, but also location. Large storms, forming in non-standard places around the globe due to an El Niño or La El Niña event, can bend the jet stream, making an unusual storm track for that time of year. The big El Niño of 1997–1998 disrupted the jet streams in the Northern Hemisphere, causing storms that were forming in the western Pacific to intensify in size, and travel at lower latitudes. In the winter of 1997–1998, this resulted in bigger west and northwest swells that slammed into the shores of Hawaii and California with massive surf.

The Southern Hemisphere encounters a displacement in its jet streams during El Niño and La El Niña event as well. During an El Niño, the polar jet can dip lower than normal, and become stronger. This can keep the large, lower latitude Southern Hemisphere winter storms farther to the south; thus, resulting in fewer and/or weaker south swells driven to areas north of the Equator like Hawaii and California during their summer (Southern Hemisphere winter).

When the summer pattern comes around, there is a shift in tropical activity as well. During El Niño years, the jet stream is stronger and tends to blow off the tops of developing hurricanes in the Atlantic, reducing the number of active hurricanes for that season. This stronger jet does not affect the eastern equatorial Pacific as much, and El Niño has an opposite effect in this region. Warmer than normal water building up in the eastern equatorial Pacific during an El Niño helps to fuel hurricane formation in that region, increasing the likelihood and strength of hurricane-driven south swells for the west coast of the US during the summer.

The PDO influences seasons as well, but is much more difficult to detect. This phenomenon occurs approximately every 20 to 30 years. During this event, an entire hemisphere (north or south) would have a warmer than normal trend, or cooler than normal trend. Since the PDO seems to occur every couple of decades, it's a hard thing to predict, and is still not fully understood.

That leaves us with two primary factors for extreme seasonal long-range surf forecast predictions:

1. **Seasonal Awareness:** Get to know how seasonal systems work in your forecast area. Every year there will be a pattern from season to season. By knowing the general seasonal pattern for your region, you'll know better how storms forming in various locations in the ocean will affect your surf. Bear in mind however that this can vary from our second factor.

2. **El Niño and La El Niña events:** There are some great on-line sources, listed in the "Resources" section of this book, regarding El Niño and La El Niña. By keeping watch every couple of months or so on these events, you can tell to some degree if the coming season could be affected by an extreme.

11

Tropical Cyclones

o o o o o o o o o o o o o o o o o o o o o o o o o o o o o o o o o

When winds are raging o'er the upper ocean
And billows wild contend with angry roar,
'Tis said, far down beneath the wild commotion
That peaceful stillness reigneth evermore.

—*Harriet Beecher Stowe*

Many of the swell-making storms we've talked about so far are fairly predictable, as they tend to follow conventional patterns such as jet streams. However, not all storms are so foreseeable. The most infamous of the unpredictable rogue storms is the tropical cyclone.

In this chapter, we'll take a look behind the science involving surf prediction for these monster storms, and close out this chapter by working through an example cyclone swell forecast from September 2002, Hurricane Hernan.

Tropical cyclones carry many names. In the North Atlantic Ocean, the Northeast Pacific Ocean east of the dateline, and the South Pacific Ocean east of 160E they are called hurricanes. In the Northwest Pacific Ocean, west of the dateline they are called typhoons. In the Southwest Pacific Ocean west of 160E and the Southeast Indian Ocean east of 90E, they are referred to as severe tropical cyclones. In the North Indian Ocean, they are called severe cyclonic storms, and in the Southwest Indian Ocean, they are called tropical cyclones.

These systems form in warm ocean waters, usually at 80 degrees Fahrenheit or more, and in deep water, approximately 150 feet or more. The Coriolis Effect that we briefly discussed in Chapter 5 is near zero at the Equator. However, it's strong enough at the 10–20 degree latitudes to spawn cyclonic formation. These latitudes are coincidentally where warmer waters reside, adding fuel to the tropical cyclones. Therefore, you'll find that most tropical cyclones don't form at the Equator where the Coriolis Effect is near zero. Instead, you'll find that most of these storms form at the 10–20 degree latitudes during hurricane season.

Requiring warm waters to fuel their existence, tropical cyclones tend to form in the summer and fall. Hurricane season for the US starts on June 1, and lasts through the end of November. During this time, the conditions are ideal for hurricane formation. However, some of the most intense hurricanes in the US have hit in the late summer and fall such as:

- Hurricane Camille, Aug. 14–22 1969
- Hurricane David, Aug. 25–Sep 7, 1979
- Hurricane Allen, Aug. 3–10, 1980
- Hurricane Juan, Oct. 6–Nov. 1, 1985
- Hurricane Hugo, Sep. 10–22, 1989
- Hurricane Andrew, Aug. 22–26, 1992
- Hurricane Gordon, Nov. 8–21, 1994
- Hurricane Opal, Nov. 29, 1995
- Hurricane Fran, Sep. 5, 1996
- Hurricane Floyd, Sep. 14–18, 1999

Each of these monster storms caused massive damage, and resulted in loss of life—truly a sad tale of the ocean's mighty strength. Although these systems can wreak havoc on coastlines, they can bring in some decent and sometimes amazing surf, provided their trajectory is favorable. Understanding these systems will enhance your forecasting during the summer and fall season when they are likely to occur.

There's an entire science dedicated to the study of tropical cyclones, and there are many areas of concern including storm surge, flooding, damage, and loss of life. For the context of this chapter however, we'll concentrate on tropical cyclones that stay far enough away to bring some surf and not the foul, adverse effects. Obviously, it would be foolhardy to attempt surfing near a hurricane.

Nevertheless, as with any storm, if these tyrants of the sea can stay many hundred or preferably a thousand or more nautical miles away from the coast, they can bring in some decent surf.

Practically all regions can get narrow escapes from hurricanes, enough to pull in some surf while the Sun stays out, and the winds remain calm. Even the east coast of the US, which is prone to hurricanes making landfall, can get some decent surf from hurricanes that stay clear of the coastline.

California is one region that rarely has newsworthy hurricanes, yet many of these storms bring in surf during the summer. The likelihood of a hurricane near California making landfall is rare. Even though an average of 18 tropical storms form over the eastern Pacific Ocean each year and around half develop into hurricanes, few of these storms hit land. In fact, no hurricane has hit the California coast since records began, but a tropical storm with 50 mph winds did come ashore at Long Beach, California on September 25, 1939, killing at least 45 people.

Eastern Pacific regions like California are spared from many damaging hurricanes for a good reason. In the equatorial Pacific, winds generally blow from east to west, pushing storms near the Equator, like hurricanes, toward the west (away from land). Some storms do turn toward the north to hit the Mexican coast, and even Baja. In addition, cold ocean water off the California coast weakens storms that make it that far north. Still, if the hurricane can travel into the California swell window, typically located around 115W (and further west), and the trajectory is greater then 290 degrees, then the angular spread is around 70 degrees, enough to throw a decent amount of swell towards the Southern California coastline. If the trajectory is more northward, then decay from angular spreading is less, resulting in stronger surf.

Most hurricanes die before they get as far west as Hawaii, but some do make it. The water around Hawaii is cooler than farther south and the storms weaken. The last hurricane to hit Hawaii was Iniki in 1992, which devastated parts of the Island of Kauai with winds estimated up to 115 mph.

Before becoming a tropical cyclone, these storms are classified as tropical systems. These systems, according to the degree of organization and maximum sustained wind speed, fall into four categories as follows:

- **Tropical disturbance, tropical wave**: Unorganized mass of thunderstorms, very little, if any, organized wind circulation.

- **Tropical depression**: Has evidence of closed wind circulation around a center with sustained winds from 20–34 knots (23–39 mph).

- **Tropical storm**: Maximum sustained winds are from 35–64 knots (40–74 mph). The storm is named once it reaches tropical storm strength.

- **Tropical Cyclone**: Maximum sustained winds exceed 64 knots (74 mph).

In the tropical cyclone group, there are five categories[1] used by the US to describe the severity as follows:

- **Category 1**: Max sustained winds of 74–95 mph (64–82 kt).
- **Category 2**: Max sustained winds of 96–110 mph (83–95 kt).
- **Category 3**: Max sustained winds of 111–130 mph (96–113 kt).
- **Category 4**: Max sustained winds of 131–155 mph (114–135 kt).
- **Category 5**: Max sustained winds of 156+ mph (136+ kt).

Like any storm we're tracking for potential swell, a tropical cyclone has to have strong enough winds, sustained over a long enough time, to create enough fetch and resultant swell energy. This means that when tracking a hurricane for surf potential, we need to track it like any other system, watching its size, duration, and direction that it's heading. But these systems can be unpredictable, making forecasts much trickier.

As a rule of thumb, the Category 1 status most often means you now have substantial swell potential; provided the storm continues to sustain itself (or grows) and, most importantly, travels on a path that could send some swell your way while staying well clear of the coastline. The Category 1 swell-making status isn't a hard and fast rule however, as some tropical storms can be surf-producers

---

1.   In the US, we use the Saffir-Simpson scale, which is slightly different from other countries like Australia.

as well. Nevertheless, for significant surf, Category 1 status serves as a good indicator.

Let's say you're located in Southern California, and you're monitoring a hurricane to the south that has increased to Category 1 and beyond. If this hurricane moves directly west, and doesn't inch its way in the least towards north, then little if any swell would come your way due to loss of angular spreading. On the other hand, if this storm moved on a WNW pattern, say at an angle of 290–300 degrees, then this would probably be enough of a northward movement to pull in some swell. Such is the case of one monster surf-generating hurricane, Hernan, which formed in the early days of September 2002.

Figure 35 is a storm track of Hurricane Hernan, provided by NOAA's National Hurricane Center.

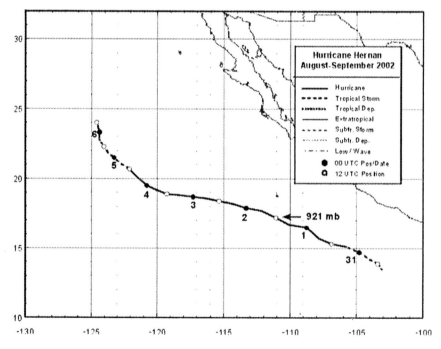

Figure 35 Hurricane Hernan Storm Track

This illustration of Hernan's storm track shows the dates, in September of 2002 (and August 31), that this storm traveled. On the 2nd, Hernan was located just within the swell window for Southern California, near the 115W longitude mark. Located near 18N, this storm was approximately 974 nautical miles away from Southern California beaches, with a swell arrival time of roughly 1.6 days.

As you may recall when we previously talked about angular spreading, the greater the angle is from the swell's direction to a forecast area, the less swell that area will get. Therefore, it is critical that when the cyclone gains enough strength to be surf-worthy, that it directs a decent enough angle of swell towards your forecast location. Hernan did just that. As we can see in Figure 35, Hernan was traveling at about 290 degrees, which was an angle of about 70 degrees from south facing beaches in Southern California.

By the 2nd, Hernan had become a category 4 hurricane with intense power and swell. With the angular spread at about 70 degrees resulting in a 30–50% loss, Hernan still threw some massive surf at Southern California that arrived less than two days later. By September 4, spots like the Wedge in Newport Beach, which were located at an ideal angle for Hernan, saw wave face heights in the range of 15–20 feet.

Let's see how this worked out using some of the calculations we've covered so far. For this exercise, we'll use the wind tables in Appendix B. This can be a great source for reference, since WAM's may not notice the rogue nature of a hurricane immediately. Hurricane reports, like those at NOAA's National Hurricane Center at http://www.nhc.noaa.gov can serve as a better resource, showing position and wind speed, eliminating the need to derive wind speeds from pressure maps using isobars or wind barbs. All we need to know are some specifics on the storm, and then use Table B-3 in Appendix B.

Hernan was quick moving—not staying put for more than 8 hours—with winds in the order of 120 knots. This fast movement is quite typical for hurricanes compared to larger ground swell systems that ride the jet streams, and is an important point to remember: hurricanes tend to have smaller fetches compared to jet stream systems with the same wind speed. If you'll recall from Chapter 6, the surf-producing properties of a fetch are wind speed, wind duration, and fetch size. Even if we had 120 kt winds, these winds need to blow long enough in the same direction to kick up some waves. Since hurricanes tend to shift course rather quickly, their wind duration in one area is limited, which in turn limits the fetch and resultant wave size.

Using Table B-3 in Appendix B, we find that for a wind-duration of eight hours (conventional for hurricane winds using this table), blowing 120-knot winds results in 70-foot swell heights with 17-second periods[2]. This is the best case for Hernan. You may want to decrease the duration to 4 hours (50-foot swell heights) depending on how un-stationary the storm is that you're tracking.

Now let's recap all the parameters we have to forecast the surf from Hernan:

- Distance to impact zone (Southern California): **974 nm**
- Decay factor (for 974 nm): **0.3** (approximately)
- Swell Height: **70 feet** (max, possibly smaller from shorter duration)
- Angular decay (70 degrees) **40% loss**
- Periods: **17 seconds**
- Shoaling factor: **1.8** (estimated)

Size works out to be, for a best-case scenario:

(70 ft swells) * (0.3 decay) = 21 feet
(21 feet) - (40% angular decay) = 12.6 feet
(12.6 feet) * (1.8 shoaling) = **22.7 foot faces (max)**

And as mentioned earlier, impact would be in less than 2 days.

Note however that this was the best-case wave height, and many breaks didn't see near as much of the swell due to increased angular spreading. In any case, using our wind estimates from Appendix B, combined with the formulas we've covered so far, you can see how we can make a surf prediction, similar to using WAM's.

Tropical cyclones however, have a nasty habit of being unpredictable. Models have gotten better at forecasting these monster storms, but since they don't follow a jet stream, they are truly the wild mavericks of the sea. The trick to forecasting surf from a tropical cyclone is persistence. Keep an eye on the system twice a

---

2.   Note that these results, based on the tables in Appendix B are rough calculations based on the Beaufort scale, and other various means we've compiled over time. As such, these may contain some margin of error.

day, and track its course. At every step along the way, calculate the swell potential from its fetch.

Cyclones can bring in some heavy and consistent surf. Caution is always advised. Furthermore, be aware of potential storm threats as well. These may be ground swell producing storms, but their reputation for destruction precedes them.

12

Logging

He who sees things grow from their beginning will have the finest view of them.

—Aristotle

Now that you've been able to predict swell arrival time, wave size, and accounted for some mitigating factors, it's time to put this all together, and track the progress of the swells you've been forecasting. There are many ways you can keep track of the swells you're predicting. I'll show you one method in this chapter based on information we've covered so far. From this information you can quickly reference your forecast data, assemble a surf schedule, and learn how your surf spots work the swells you've been tracking.

This chapter provides a worksheet tool to log your surf predictions, as well as an example of how this is used. Figure 36 shows a blank worksheet, and Figure 37 shows an example of this tool.

As you forecast a swell, log the data and calculation results on a line in this worksheet. After the swell arrives, you can then compare your forecast with the actual results. By doing this with numerous swells, you'll gain a better understanding of how swells forming in various locations will affect the surf at your favorite breaks.

The columns in this worksheet are:

- **Date**: This is the date that you forecasted the swell.
- **Location**: This is the location of the fetch.

- **Swell Period**: Use this as the peak wave period of the swell.

- **Distance**: This is the distance to the fetch, in nautical miles that we discussed in Chapter 6.

- **Arrival Date**: The swell will arrive on this day, based on your calculations.

- **Swell Height**: This is the maximum swell height (significant wave height) of the storm you are tracking.

- **Angle**: This is the angle of the incoming swell, as discussed in Chapter 3.

- **Decay Factor**: This is the decay factor discussed in Chapter 7.

- **Angular Decay**: This is the percentage of decay based on the angular spreading of the swell (from Chapters 7 and 8).

- **Arrival Size**: This is how big the swell height of the waves should be when they arrive at the beach.

- **Shoaling**: This is the shoaling factor we discussed in Chapters 7 and 8. This can be a combination of shoaling and refraction. So feel free to use modified versions of our shoaling factors that best fit the surf spots you're forecasting.

- **Face Height**: This is the face height, which is the arrival size multiplied by the shoaling factor.

Now let's run through our example surf log in Figure 37 to see how this all comes together.

The first thing you record for any swell is the date that you predicted it. Bear in mind that if you are using long-range models, you may want to add the prediction time to this date. For instance, looking at our example, in line 1, the forecast date is 1-Sep. If this was the day you were predicting the swell, and you based your calculations on a 24-hour model, then you may want to label this date as 2-Sep.

Next, record the location of the leading edge of the storm's fetch. You can log this in coordinates as in the example, or use some other reference that is familiar to you. For instance, you might want to write something like "30 degrees east of New Zealand" instead of the 30S, 150W that is used in our example. Use whatever you feel comfortable with so you can refer back to this the next time you predict a swell in this region.

The next column is for the swell period. Remember that the bigger period waves will travel faster, and is what our calculations so far have been based on. Therefore, use the highest period of the storm fetch you are tracking.

Then, record the distance in the "Distance" column.

Next, record the arrival date you derived from your calculations. Place this in the "Arrival Date" column.

The remaining columns relate to the same swell, but are pertinent to the size of the expected waves.

In the "Swell Height" column, place the significant wave height of the fetch. Remember that we're calculating the biggest waves with the longest periods, so make sure this has the maximum wave height of the fetch.

The "Decay Factor" column lists the decay factor for this storm, as we discussed in Chapter 7.

Similarly, record the percentage of decay you expect from the angular spread of the swell as discussed in Chapters 7 and 8, and place this in the "Angular Decay" column.

Now it's time for the moment of truth: the "Arrival Size". This result is obtained by multiplying the decay factor to the swell height, then subtracting angular decay. The formula is:

A = Arrival Size
SH = Swell Height
DF = Decay Factor
AD = Angular Decay

A = SH * DF
A = A - AD

Lastly, multiply the shoaling factor to the arrival size to achieve an estimated face height:

Face Height = A * Shoaling

Bear in mind that shoaling factors need to be adjusted for your particular breaks since this factor relies on not just the period of the swell, but bathymetry affecting shoaling and refraction as well.

Now that you've recorded the swells, it's time to see if they'll be all you expected. This is the topic of our next chapter, "Now Casts", where we'll look at confirmation.

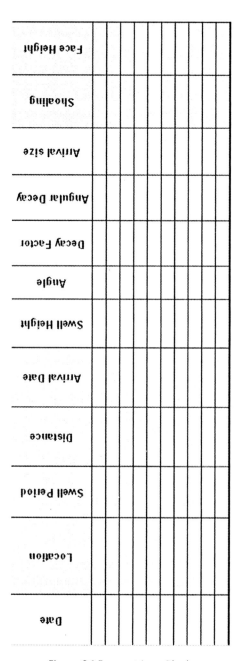

Figure 36 Forecast Log, Blank

Date	Location	Swell Period	Distance	Arrival Date	Swell Height	Angle	Decay Factor	Angular Decay	Arrival size	Shoaling	Face Height
1-Sep	30S. 150W	16	4249 nm	8-Sep	25	210	0.14	0%	3.5	1.8	6.3
3-Sep	30S. 180W	18	5206 nm	12-Sep	38	230	0.13	10%	4.4	1.85	8.1
6-Sep	40N. 170W	17	2484 nm	10-Sep	30	290	0.16	15%	4	1.8	7.2
8-Sep	30N. 165W	19	2384 nm	11-Sep	40	280	0.16	5%	6	1.85	11.1
9-Sep	35N. 140W	10	1088 nm	12-Sep	15	275	0.28	0%	4.2	1.2	5.0

Figure 37 Forecast Log, Example

13

Now Casts

"For all at last return to the sea—to Oceanus, the ocean river, like the ever-flowing stream of time, the beginning and the end."

—*Rachel Carson*

You've diligently tracked a swell heading to your favorite surf spot. For days, possibly a week or more, you've tracked the progress of this system. Then the day comes when it's time to hit the surf, and ride the energy that originated a thousand or more miles away. But how do you know this swell is all it's cracked up to be? You could drive down to the beach, and like Christmas morning, see if there's a long-awaited present ready to be opened. If you live a block or two from the coast, this would probably be your best way to see if Mother Nature worked in your favor. But what if you don't have the luxury of being so close to the coastline?

Thanks to the technology of the Internet, and a variety of free, publicly available resources, you can get swell confirmation, also known as a "Now Cast" before making the trip for your anticipated session.

There are two primary sources for Now Cast data:

1. Buoy data
2. Swell models

There are a number of buoy resources for regions around the globe, some of which are listed in the "Resources" section near the end of this book. One of those resources, The National Data Buoy Center (NDBC) located on the Internet at http://www.ndbc.noaa.gov, deploys buoys for the coastlines of the US, Hawaii, Caribbean, and parts of Europe. We talked briefly about these buoys in Chapter 5 when looking at coastal winds. In this chapter, we'll use the NDBC buoys to see what's happening close to your favorite surf spots.

Figure 38 shows one of the many buoy maps you can access at the NDBC web site.

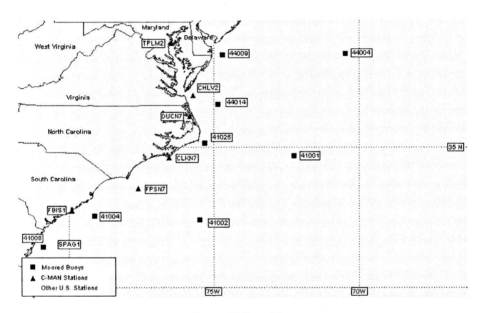

Figure 38 Buoy Map

This particular buoy map shows the central portion of the east coast of the US. Clicking on a buoy number will display a buoy report, just like the ones we used in Chapter 5 when discussing winds. Notice how there are buoys along the coast, and some farther out. Using a combination of these buoys, we can track the arrival of a swell within hours of it hitting the coast.

For instance, let's say that you wanted to track an easterly swell coming in for the Carolinas. You could watch activity on buoy 41002, and calculate its distance and arrival time using the great circle measurements we discussed in Chapter 6. Depending on the periods of the swell, you could gauge arrival to the coast, giving you a near-term forecast and confirmation.

As this swell approached the coast, you could check it against buoy number 41004, located off the coast of South Carolina. However, this particular buoy is 41 nautical miles away from the coast. There will inevitably be some decay in energy, refraction, and other mitigating factors as the swell approaches the coastline. Still, these near-shore buoys can work as great indicators for swell confirmation.

The NDBC provides reports for five types of buoys, all of which we can see on the buoy map example in Figure 38:

1. **Moored Buoys**: The buoys we previously mentioned (41002, and 41004) fall into this category. These have the most data, and are often thought of as the weather sentinels of the sea. NDBC's moored buoys measure and transmit barometric pressure; wind direction, speed, and gust; air and sea temperature, and wave energy data.

2. **C-MAN Stations**: C-MAN stands for Coastal-Marine Automated Network. These smaller stations, located very close to shore, are carryovers from the 1980s. These provide some weather data, but unfortunately, don't usually provide any wave data.

3. **Drifting Buoys**: As its name implies, these buoys drift around, staying primarily near one location. Data is very limited from these buoys.

4. **DART Buoys**: DART stands for Deep Ocean Assessment and Reporting of Tsunamis (you would think it would be DOART, but it's not, it's DART). These buoys participate in an ongoing effort to maintain and improve the capability for the early detection and real-time reporting of tsunamis in the open ocean.

5. **Other Stations**: This category is a variety of stations like Navy towers, that don't fall into any other category. Depending on the station, you may or may not find wave data.

In Chapter 5, we briefly talked about the buoy data, and how you can read conditions from the tables provided in each NDBC buoy report. However, there are graphical representations of the data as well. To access these, you need to click on icons located next to summary data like that shown in Figure 39.

Conditions at 41004 as of (11:00 am EDT) 1500 GMT on 10/15/2003:

	Wind Direction (WDIR):	NW (320 deg true)
	Wind Speed (WSPD):	17.5 kts
	Wind Gust (GST):	21.4 kts
	Wave Height (WVHT):	4.9 ft
	Dominant Wave Period (DPD):	5 sec
	Atmospheric Pressure (PRES):	29.96 in
	Pressure Tendency (PTDY):	+0.07 in (Rising)
	Air Temperature (ATMP):	65.7 °F
	Water Temperature (WTMP):	77.7 °F
	Dew Point (DEWP):	48.2 °F

Figure 39 Buoy Summary for Buoy 41004

From this summary, we can quickly see the current readings. And, if you click on the icon next to each item, you will see a graphical representation of the historic data for that item. For instance, if you were to click on the icon next to "Wave Height" you would see a graph like that shown in Figure 40.

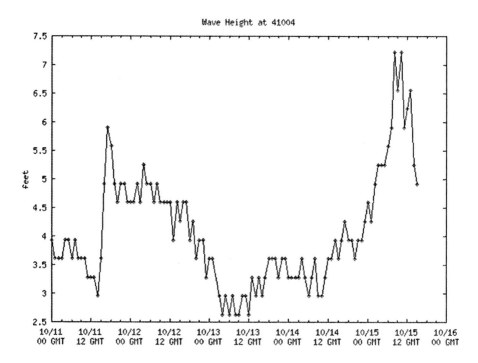

Figure 40 Wave Height at Buoy 41004

This particular graph shows us the wave heights (Y-axis referenced on the left hand side of the graph) over the past few days (X-axis referenced on the bottom). From this example, we can see that the wave size picked up, but is now on the way down.

By getting to know buoys close to your forecast region, you can obtain Now Cast data to provide swell confirmation. It may take some practice, but with time, you can hone this skill, watching various swells hit nearby buoys, then comparing that to near term conditions, as well as prior forecasts.

The second type of Now Cast data source is the swell model. This type of model shouldn't be confused with WAM's, which show predictions. Swell models, are initialized from buoy data, and provide an estimate, with fair amount of accuracy, of the events currently taking place along the coast.

If you surf along the California coast, you can access free swell models at the web site for The Coastal Data Information Program (CDIP) of Scripps Institution of Oceanography at http://cdip.ucsd.edu/ Unfortunately, these models are not yet available for other regions and are limited right now to the California coast.

Figure 31 in Chapter 8 shows an example swell model for Southern California from the CDIP. Similar to WAM's, the swell models use a color scheme as a reference key. This key is located at either the top or bottom of the model, showing the wave size along the coast. Note that this is swell height. The actual face height will tend to be bigger once you factor in shoaling and refraction (from Chapters 7 and 8).

Besides showing the wave size, the CDIP swell models also show information on the wave spectrum. There are two points of interest here. The first is the "Deep Water Swell" information shown in the upper right corner of the model. This tells us the primary swell of the spectrum from the north and south.

The second aspect of the spectrum data is the graphical representation of the spectrum shown in the bottom left of the model. This shows the angles of the swell, and their periods. This can give you, at a glance, a quick idea of what kind of swell is in the water.

From the CDIP swell models then, we can see three things:

1. How big it is from the color coding

2. The synopsis of swell angles and size in the "Deep Water Swell" data

3. A graphical representation of the swell spectrum

Bear in mind however that this data is an estimate based on data retrieved from a single buoy. In the case of the Southern California swell model, this data is initialized from the CDIP Harvest Buoy located off Point Conception, which is located north of the model area. Still, these models have been refined over time to get it right, and they usually do. It's a great way to see a simulation of what's happening.

14

Hazards

o o o o o o o o o o o o o o o o o o o o o o o o o o o o o o o o

Never expose yourself unnecessarily to danger; a miracle may not save you…and if it does, it will be deducted from your share of luck or merit.

—*The Talmud*

Surf forecasting involves more than foreseeing the enjoyment that awaits you in the coastal waters. Forecasting also requires knowledge of hazards and dangerous conditions, giving you advance notice so you can survive in good health to surf another day.

In this chapter we'll take a look at some of the more common hazards associated with ocean water sports, and how to forecast these conditions. These include:

- Size, impact, and consistency
- Alongshore currents (also known as longshore currents and along shore currents)
- Rip currents (commonly called rip tides)
- Bacteria
- Postings and flags

Size, Impact, and Consistency

Combining your surfing skill level with your forecasts is a great amalgamation. One of the primary reasons I started the WaveCast® service many years ago was so that I could prepare for sessions that were within my skill and comfort zone, where I knew I would have a great time and walk away unscathed.

There is no shame in knowing your limits, and having alternative plans on days where Mother Ocean has the home-court advantage. It's the experienced forecaster and skilled water sport enthusiast who can judge with accuracy his or her time in the water.

Much of the hazard surrounding size, impact, and consistency is common sense. Knowing how big waves will be tells you of impending danger from the release of massive quantities of energy. The impact of these waves can not only break bones, or knock the wind out of you, but adding consistency to the mix, you may fall victim to the merciless sea.

Not all swells are good swells. Many of the bigger swells that hit a coast do so from a direct path to the shoreline. This can increase the likelihood of closed out sets—having far more power—raising the likelihood of getting shot over the falls, encountering lengthy hold-downs, and getting churned in the soup of these pile-driving waves.

Know your limits, and don't be ashamed of them. Know how your skill set (and sense of reason) will coexist with the swells you are forecasting.

Alongshore Currents

Alongshore currents are quite simply currents that flow along the shore. As waves move toward the shoreline at an angle, an alongshore current flowing parallel to the beach develops. Depending on the environmental conditions, alongshore currents vary in speed, but rarely do they exceed one knot.

Alongshore currents are most common along straight beaches. The speed of the current increases from:

- The height of the breaking waves.
- Decreasing wave periods with increased consistency.
- Increasing angle of the waves to the beach.
- Increasing beach slopes.

Consistent surf, combined with big waves, and a swell angle not directly facing the beach, is a formula for an alongshore current. Knowing that a swell will bring in these conditions can alert you of this danger.

This hazard is noticeable as you watch the surf zone near the shore. You may see dirty water from sediment stirred up from an alongshore current. In addition, you will notice a drift to one direction near the shore. For instance, on a big day with an alongshore current, you might watch surfers paddle straight out, but end up somewhat farther down the coast once they make it outside (*if* they make it outside).

The hazard of alongshore currents is critically important when you are planning a session near piers, jetty's, or other obstacles that you could drift into. If you do attempt to go out on a day with an alongshore current, caution is highly advised. Nevertheless, if you do, remember that you will inevitably drift with this current; therefore, you need to plan your paddle to the outside accordingly.

If you are already in the water, and realize you are caught in an alongshore current, and are approaching a structure such as a pier or jetty, the best advice is to get out of the water as soon as possible, and go back out further up the coast, far away from obstacles that you could drift in to. Then again, if the alongshore current is strong, perhaps you should consider staying out of the water, and do something else for the day.

Rip Currents

Rip currents, often referred to as rip tides, are the most common natural hazard encountered in the surf zone, aside from monster backbreaking waves. Rip currents only become life threatening under certain combinations of beach shape, tide, wind, and wave conditions. Although some beaches are more prone to rip currents than others are, rip currents have been documented in almost every coastal location around the globe, including the Great Lakes in the US. These currents are commonly found near jetties, groins, piers, breaks in sand bars, and inlets.

NOAA's National Weather Service estimates that approximately 100 people fall victim to rip currents along US waters each year, and cause several hundred more deaths globally each year. Statistics[1] reveal that rip currents account for nearly 80 percent of all surf-related rescues each year, rank third among average yearly hazard fatalities, and cause more average deaths per year than lightning, tornadoes, hurricanes, winter and cold.

A rip current is a relatively small-scale surf-zone current that flows away from the beach. These currents form as waves disperse along the beach causing water to become trapped between the beach and a sand bar or other underwater structure. Then due to gravity, the trapped water flows back towards the sea. As the water flows away from the beach, it will seek a path of least resistance, such as a break in a sand bar. This flow of water away from the beach is a rip current.

Rip currents can be predicted to a certain degree. Although rip currents could occur on any given day at practically any beach around the world, there are certain conditions that make them more likely. The biggest factor is large surf. Consistent breaking waves will push more water up on the beach; thereby, more water can get trapped as a result. Strong onshore winds also play a similar role.

You can predict the likelihood of rip currents when there is a significant swell coming in, and/or there will be strong on-shore winds. Also, note that some breaks are more prone to rip currents than others are. If you're unfamiliar with rip currents for your favorite surf spots, don't be afraid to ask someone like a lifeguard about the potentials for rip currents in that area. There is no harm in asking a simple question that could save your life someday.

Once at the beach, rip currents may be hard to detect, but there are some telltale signs:

1. If the water at the beach is relatively clear, a rip current may appear darker than the rest of the water around it.

2. Areas where waves are not breaking are flanked by breaking waves, which increases the likelihood of a rip current in that area. Waves coming in on either side of a calmer spot will find a path of least resistance through the calmer water, allowing the dispersed water to flow back to the sea through this calm area; thus, creating a rip current.

3. There may be seaweed or the water itself seen flowing away from the beach in a rip current.

---

1.   Per NOAA News http://www.noaanews.noaa.gov/magazine/stories/mag48.htm

4. If the water is roughed up by heavy surf, then there may be foam along the neck of the rip current (the channel where the water flows out to sea).

An additional tip for spotting rip currents once you are at the beach is to look at the water with polarized sunglasses. This will reduce the glare and allow you to see rip conditions more readily.

If you are caught in a rip current, don't panic, and do not attempt to swim or paddle directly to shore. You'll merely be swimming against the current, which could be as great as 5 kt or more. Instead, swim or paddle parallel to the beach until you are out of the rip current, then paddle back to shore.

For more information on rip currents, I highly recommend the following article from NOAA News, from which, parts of this discussion were excerpt: http://www.noaanews.noaa.gov/magazine/stories/mag48.htm

Bacteria

One of the lesser-recognized hazards of ocean water sports is the quality of the water. What may look innocuous could make you nauseous. We need to remember that the ocean is unfortunately a dumping ground where natural and man-made waterways allow water to flow off land, and spill into the surf zone. This is especially important after a rain when animal waste, fertilizer from yards, and other debris in dry riverbeds, flood channels, and storm drains gets flushed to the sea. Then there are those unforeseen times when septic tanks fail, or sewage plants have a breech.

Many bacteria reports are online, some of which are listed in the "Resources" section near the end of this book. These will usually test for coliform and enterococcus. Contaminated water may contain these bacteria, viruses, and other organisms, which can cause flu-like symptoms including vomiting, fever, diarrhea, skin rashes and sinus or ear infections.

To forecast bacteria hazards, you can rely on a couple of things:

1. If there is going to be, or has been rain, bacteria becomes inevitable. Rain increases the likelihood of increased bacteria from runoff. It is advisable to avoid the water for at least 72 hours after the rain has

stopped, provided bacteria reports agree with the dissipation of contamination.

2. Keep track of the water quality monitoring for your region. Be aware of areas prone to contamination as well as those that aren't. In addition, always keep a watch for reports on sewage spills and the like.

Postings and Flags

Even though you can forecast some ocean hazards, it's good to be aware of postings and flags once you arrive at the beach. Many public beaches around the world have adopted warning signs and flags as indicators of hazardous conditions.

Although not fully adopted around the world, the United States Lifesaving Association has proposed the following standard for flags at beaches, some of which are in wide use today, especially throughout the US:

- **Green Flag:** Low Hazard (small surf, light currents, and clean water)

- **Yellow Flag:** Moderate Hazard (moderate surf and/or strong currents)

- **Red Flag**: High Hazard (high surf and/or very strong currents and/or contaminated water advisory)

- **Red Flag over Red Flag:** Water is closed to public contact. (One red flag flown above a second red flag.)

- **Purple Flag:** Marine pests present (e.g., jellyfish, stingrays, Portuguese man-o-war)—Note: This is not intended to be used to notify the presence of sharks. If water is closed or hazardous due to the presence of sharks, red flags are used.

- **Yellow with Black Ball Flag:** Surfing prohibited—Note: According to local regulation, this may include a variety of defined surf riding devices.

- **Black Flag:** Surfing permitted

- **Checkered Flag:** Use Area Boundary (example: boundary of a swimming and surfing area)

- **Red over Yellow Flag:** Protected Area Boundary (end of lifeguard protection)

Additionally, many areas have adopted warning signs that are clearly written, usually in English and other languages common to that area.

15

Water Temperature

o o o o o o o o o o o o o o o o o o o o o o o o o o o o o o o o o o o

It doesn't make a difference what temperature a room is, it's always room temperature.

—*Steven Wright*

You've been watching a swell headed your way for over a week or more and confirmed its arrival. Now it's time to pull the appropriate board out of your quiver, strap it to your racks, and drive down to the beach. But, if you don't live in a tropical climate, then there is one vital piece of gear you may need: a wetsuit. Furthermore, which one should you bring? Can you expect to wear a short john, spring suit, or just trunk it? Or is this going to be a full suit day with booties?

If you live in areas prone to cold water like California or the east coast of the US, you may ask yourself this question. After all, if you ever surfed these areas in the summertime, you might have gotten an unpleasant bone chilling surprise one day when entering the water under-suited. The week before your session the water may have been 70 F, or more. Now, even though it's the middle of summer, the water may have dipped to a nippy 60 F.

Such was the case this past year (2003) when temperatures at Daytona Beach, Florida in July were below 70 degrees on numerous days with some days in the mid 60's. This was far below the normal water temperatures that often reach the 80 degree mark, or slightly higher during that time of year.

Water temperature is an element that is somewhat difficult to forecast for the long term, but is fairly easy to gauge for the short term. Before you head out for that long awaited session, you can check the current water temperatures from a variety of sources, including some of our WaveCast® reports at wetsand.com. But how do you know if the swell arriving next week may encounter some colder than normal water? And how do you know if you'll need a thicker wetsuit for the coming winter?

That's not an easy question to answer, but there are long-term trends to look for, and short term trends as well that can give you a reasonable forecast of what to expect.

For long-term trends, you can monitor El Niño and La Niña events, which would affect the water temperature for a season. If you'll recall from our discussion on seasonal trends in Chapter 10, El Niño and La Niña years cause ocean water temperature fluctuations around the globe. For instance, during an El Niño year the waters will be warmer in the eastern portion of the Pacific, yet colder during a La Niña year.

For short-term trends, you can be on the lookout for sudden anomalies in water temperature. The most prevalent short-term anomaly is upwelling—common in areas prone to cold water like California and the east coast of the US. Upwelling is also the reason for those chilly days at Daytona Beach in July 2003.

Upwelling is an interesting phenomenon, and occurs rather frequently. Under normal conditions, warm water stays at the ocean surface. During the summer, the Sun beats down on the water, and warms it. The surface of the water is the warmest since molecules of warm water are farther apart than molecules of cold water, making warm water less dense. Cold water, whose molecules are closer together, is denser, so it sinks to the bottom. This layering of warm water at the surface and colder water towards the bottom is called stratification.

So why would this change? It makes sense from knowing this basic principle of stratification and rudimentary physics that the warmer the sunlight, the warmer the water, at least on the surface where the Sun can penetrate its energy. Therefore, summer should have warmer water, and winter should have colder water. Nevertheless, this can change if your area is susceptible to upwelling.

In upwelling, we need to remember that the warm water is at the surface, not deep underneath. If the cold water were to rise (upwell), it would replace the warm water, and really chill things off. What causes the cold water to rise up and replace the warmer water during an upwelling is wind from the proper direction.

When the wind blows parallel to the coast, the surface water can be moved away from the coast. If the warm surface water found along the coast during the summer is moved away from the coast by winds, colder water from beneath the surface rises up and takes its place.

The amazing thing about an upwelling is that you might think winds would push all the water, or at least most of the water, towards the shore. In California, upwelling is caused from northwest winds paralleling the coast. On the east coast, it is usually winds from the southwest. Due to the Coriolis Effect—which as mentioned in Chapter 5 is due to the rotation of the Earth—an effect known as Ekman Transport comes into play.

Ekman Transport will move the surface water at roughly a 90-degree angle from the direction of the wind. This causes the warm surface water to be pulled away from the coast, leaving room for the colder water underneath to come up to replace it.

To summarize, winds paralleling a coast can draw the warm surface water away from the coast. Once the surface water is drawn away, the cold water underneath wells up to replace the void.

It's important to note that the Coriolis Effect, which is responsible for the Ekman Transport—and hence the nature of upwelling from winds paralleling a coast—is weakest near the Equator. The Coriolis Effect is stronger the farther away you travel from the Equator. As such, upwelling is more likely to occur in latitudes greater than 20 degrees.

Upwelling events typically take place during the summer months (May-September in the Northern Hemisphere, December-March in the Southern Hemisphere).

In California, an upwelling is inevitable if the coast sees winds from the northwest for a long enough time, usually a couple days of steady, nonstop winds. Strong winds during an upwelling can add insult to injury. If you'll recall from our earlier discussion on sea breezes in Chapter 5, the land is warmed from the

Sun's heat, and the ocean remains cooler. If the ocean water is cooler than normal, the winds tend to be stronger. If these winds continue to blow, they will inevitably push the surface water away, allowing the cold water from the deep to rise and take its place. Now you have even colder water, which could make for a stronger sea breeze pattern, which brings us back to stronger winds that could intensify the upwelling. It can be a vicious cycle if the initial upwelling is great.

When it comes to forecasting temperature from a general perspective, there are some basic principles to note:

1. Wintertime will inevitably have colder water, and is likely to stay on a moderate fluctuation since the Sun will not have a chance to warm the surface water as much.

2. Summertime can have inevitably warmer water, but is susceptible to upwelling (item 3).

3. Upwelling could affect summer water temperatures drastically, and needs to be monitored. Look for winds paralleling a coastline and blowing continuously for at least one to two days. This is mainly for regions at or greater than 20 degrees latitude.

4. El Niño and La Niña years can have abnormally warmer or colder water depending on the equatorial water mass containing the anomalous temperatures (Chapter 10). During an El Niño year, the waters will be warmer in the eastern portion of the Pacific, yet colder during a La Niña year. Other regions have different effects depending on the placement of the equatorial warm water mass relative to their location.

To check out the current water temperatures, you can use a variety of sources in the WaveCast® reports on wetsand.com, as well as those listed in the "Resources" section of this book. These include accessing buoys like those at the NDBC at http://www.ndbc.noaa.gov/

The buoy reports at the NDBC can tell you more than just the current water temperature. They can also tell you the trend in temperature for the past five days. By reviewing the latest trend in temperatures up and down the coast, you could spot an upwelling underway. Additionally, you can see if the trend in temperature is dropping, or rising.

To access the time plots for temperature (and other data) from the NDBC buoys, you can click on the summary icons in the buoy report as shown in Figure 41.

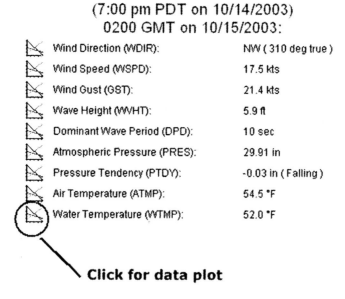

**Conditions at 46042 as of
(7:00 pm PDT on 10/14/2003)
0200 GMT on 10/15/2003:**

	Wind Direction (WDIR):	NW (310 deg true)
	Wind Speed (WSPD):	17.5 kts
	Wind Gust (GST):	21.4 kts
	Wave Height (WVHT):	5.9 ft
	Dominant Wave Period (DPD):	10 sec
	Atmospheric Pressure (PRES):	29.91 in
	Pressure Tendency (PTDY):	-0.03 in (Falling)
	Air Temperature (ATMP):	54.5 °F
	Water Temperature (WTMP):	52.0 °F

Click for data plot

Figure 41 Temperature Plot Link in Buoy Report

Clicking on this icon will give you a plot like that shown in Figure 42.

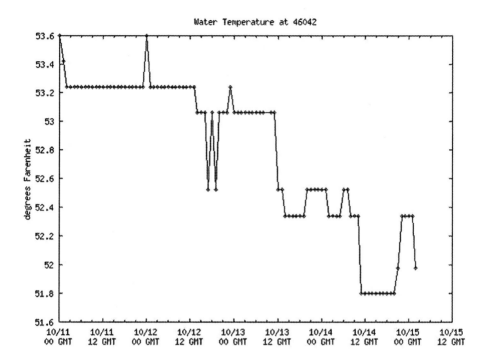

Figure 42 Plot of Water Temps from Buoy Report

In our example plot, we can see water temperatures at this buoy for the past few days. This example shows a downward trend in water temperatures, which could signal an upwelling, or just cold water for the time of year: October. If you observed on the buoy reports that wind had been paralleling the coast for the past few days, then it is more than likely that upwelling is causing the change in water temperature. If so, areas further downwind from this location could soon feel the colder water effect.

Also, when reading buoy reports for water temperature, wind, or other data, always bear in mind that the buoys are mostly off shore by about 20 miles or more. This brings us to one primary principle of surf forecasting: experience. Get to know your surf spots—how they work with the elements of Mother Nature, and the indicators available for you to monitor close-proximity results.

Practice makes perfect, or at least gets you close to it anyway.

16

Parting Words

○ ○
The goal of life is living in agreement with nature.

—Zeno (335 BC–264 BC)

Well, that's surf forecasting in a nutshell, mostly learned through the school of hard knocks, diligence, experience, and a touch of basic physics. Although this book didn't go in depth into the sciences involving oceanography and wave physics, I felt as though we covered enough of the basics to show surf forecasting from a simple yet accurate perspective.

Sure—the calculations in this book won't estimate every nuance of ocean surface waves, nor will they get us within the exact minute of wave arrival. From my personal experience, when it comes to planning a good session, and taking a day or two off from work, these intricacies aren't necessary. It's a matter of knowing if today, tomorrow, or next week may be worth spending the time to do nothing else but soak up as much stoke as possible. And that's what it all boils down to.

When I think of all the trouble in the world today, with so many people in despair, some harboring hatred, and others dieing from hunger and disease, my heart feels heavy. In my escape, I often drift back to my last session, remembering the last wave I caught, the warmth of the Sun, and the calmness of the water that surrounded me. Although my empathy never wanes for those less fortunate, and my sympathy remains for those with hostilities and the wars they wage, I find comfort in knowing how fortunate I am to be able to participate with nature, and enjoy the gift of life.

If only more people could see the joy that our world can bring—even in the simplest of pleasures like watching the Sun set across the ocean's horizon, hearing the rhythmic crash of waves on the shore, and breathing the moist salt air while lying on a warm, dry, sandy beach. If only everyone could see the peace that surrounds us all, I feel this world would be a better place.

I find joy and harmony with the ocean. But it's not all by chance. The ocean can be unforgiving with intense and fatal power. At other times, it can seem like a sleeping giant. Knowing how to forecast surfing conditions, and plan the *perfect* session, I'm able to participate with Mother Nature on her terms—maximizing my time in this circle of life with as many enjoyable moments as possible.

My hope is that this book and our forecasting service can bring you the joy, happiness, and thrills that our great oceans offer while at the same time keeping you safe to enjoy as many days as possible in the surf zone. Life is a venture, with many road stops of happiness and enjoyment on its long and winding road. With the knowledge of surf forecasting, you can pick and choose those stops along the way.

The journey does not end here. The WaveCast® service will continue as long as possible to provide you with free surf forecasts from as many regions as possible, and strive to provide you with the best of resources—like the information in this book—to help you make the most of your time. Time is the most valuable asset we can possess, and one to be invested well.

To continue our voyage through the science of surf forecasting, and planning the *perfect* sessions, we've dedicated a small portion of our web site to this book, located at: http://wavecast.com/guide

Feel free to stop by, check out any revisions or corrections for this book, drop us a line, use our distance calculator, and as always, check out our free surf reports for your region.

Thank you for making the WaveCast® service at WetSand such a success. It is with the deepest sincerity that myself, and everyone at WetSand WaveCast®, wish you the best of sessions, and stoke unlimited.

Until our next report, take care, be safe, enjoy life, and watch the horizon...

Nathan Todd Cool

Resources

o o o o o o o o o o o o o o o o o o o o o o o o o o o o o o o o o

Knowledge is of two kinds. We know a subject ourselves, or we know where we can find information on it.

—*Samuel Johnson*

The following are a handful of resources that were mentioned throughout this book. These are free and publicly available for everyone to use.

Updates, Information, and Feedback

http://wavecast.com/guide

Great Circle Calculators

http://wavecast.com/guide
http://www.argray.org/dist/
http://www.fcc.gov/mb/audio/bickel/distance.html

Free WaveCast® Reports at WetSand

http://www.wetsand.com/wavecast/

Pressure Maps:

http://virga.sfsu.edu/
http://www.mpc.ncep.noaa.gov/
http://www.nws.noaa.gov/
http://www.weather.com/

Weather Reports:

http://www.nws.noaa.gov/
http://www.weather.com/
http://www.intellicast.com/
http://www.wunderground.com/
http://wwwa.accuweather.com/

Coastal Eddies:

http://www.wrh.noaa.gov/Sandiego/eddy.html
http://airsea-www.jpl.nasa.gov/cos/california/ocean_eddies.html
http://cimss.ssec.wisc.edu/goes/misc/980616.html
http://www2.faa.gov/ats/hhrafss/influences.htm
http://squall.sfsu.edu/crws/specials/catalina_eddy_951013/
cateddy_951013.html

WAM's

https://www.fnmoc.navy.mil/PUBLIC/
http://polar.wwb.noaa.gov/waves/main_text.html
http://facs.scripps.edu/surf/gblpac.html

Information on El Niño and La Niña

http://www.elnino.noaa.gov/
http://www.pmel.noaa.gov/tao/elnino/el-nino-story.html
http://www.ogp.noaa.gov/enso/

Time and Date

http://www.timeanddate.com/worldclock/
http://www.time.gov

Buoys

NDBC (US, Hawaii, Caribbean, and more): http://www.ndbc.noaa.gov/
California summary: http://facs.scripps.edu/surf/buoylist.html
Australia: http://www.coastaldata.transport.wa.gov.au/
 and:
http://www.env.qld.gov.au/environmental_management/coast_and_oceans/
waves_and_tides/wave_monitoring/

Swell Models

http://cdip.ucsd.edu/cdip_htmls/models.shtml

Hurricanes and Cyclones

http://www.nhc.noaa.gov/
http://www.nhc.noaa.gov/aboutrsmc.shtml
http://www.solar.ifa.hawaii.edu/Tropical/
http://twister.sbs.ohio-state.edu/tropical.html
http://www.npmoc.navy.mil/jtwc.html
http://www.ns.ec.gc.ca/weather/hurricane/

Water Temperatures

California coast: http://cdip.ucsd.edu/cgi-bin/synopsis.sh
From Buoys: http://www.ndbc.noaa.gov/
Other: http://www.nodc.noaa.gov/dsdt/cwtg/

Water Quality

http://www.wetsand.com/wavecast/waterquality.htm
http://www.healthebay.org/
http://www.epa.gov/ost/beaches/
http://www.surfrider.org/

Glossary

Alongshore current: A current located in the surf zone, moving generally parallel to the shoreline, generated by waves breaking at an angle with the shoreline, also called the longshore current.

Angular Spreading: Spreading of waves in space due to differences in direction of wave propagation.

Angular-Spreading Factor: Fraction by which the estimated energy of waves leaving the swell generation area is multiplied to obtain the forecast wave energy at a distant point, after reduction due to angular spreading.

Bathymetry: The measurement of depths of water in oceans, seas and lakes; also the information derived from such measurements.

Beaufort Number (Beaufort Scale): Categorization of wind speed based on visual state of the sea or land effects.

Breaker: A wave that has reached maximum steepness and is breaking.

Chop: Short-crested waves that spring up following onset of a moderate breeze, and break readily at the crest.

Coriolis Effect: Force due to the Earth's rotation, capable of generating currents. It causes moving bodies to be deflected to the right in the Northern Hemisphere and to the left in the Southern Hemisphere. The force is proportional to the speed and latitude of the moving object. It is zero at the equator and maximum at the poles.

Crest: The highest point on a wave.

Deep Water Wave: A wave for which water depth is greater than one half the wave length.

Dispersion: The tendency of longer waves to travel faster than shorter waves due to the proportionality between wave phase speed and wavelength.

Diurnal: Relating to or occurring in a 24-hour period; daily

Eddy: A current of air, water, or any fluid, forming on the side of the main current, especially one moving in a circle; in extreme cases a whirlpool.

Ekman Transport: The net flow of water to the right of the wind in the Northern Hemisphere and to the left of the wind in the Southern Hemisphere, which arises because of the Coriolis Effect.

ETA: Estimated time of arrival.

Fetch: The uninterrupted distance over which the wind blows (measured in the direction of the wind) without a significant change of direction.

Fully Developed Sea: A sea state in which waves have reached maximum energy. Additional energy added to the spectrum is dissipated by wave breaking.

GMT (Greenwich Mean Time): This is the time at the zero degree meridian crossing through Greenwich, England.

GPS: Global positioning system.

Great Circle: An imaginary circle on the surface of a sphere whose plane passes through the center of the sphere. It's also the actual path that a craft (or storm) takes across the globe.

Groin: Narrow, roughly shore-normal structure built to reduce alongshore currents, and/or to trap and retain littoral material. Most groins are made of timber or rock and extend from a seawall, or the backshore, well onto the foreshore and rarely even further offshore.

Jetty: On open seacoasts, a structure extending into a body of water, which is designed to prevent shoaling of a channel by littoral materials and to direct and confine the stream or tidal flow. Jetties are typically built at the mouths of rivers or tidal inlets to help deepen and stabilize a channel.

Kentucky Windage: An estimate of the modified point of aim required to compensate for wind or for target movement. Slang for a rough estimate.

Knot: A unit of speed equal to one nautical mile per hour.

Longshore current: A current located in the surf zone, moving generally parallel to the shoreline, generated by waves breaking at an angle with the shoreline, also called the alongshore current.

Leeward: The direction toward which the wind and waves are going.

Pressure Gradient: The change in pressure over a given distance at a given time, also called "grads".

Mean Wave Direction: Primary swell direction, technically speaking it's the overall direction in degrees obtained by averaging the mean wave angle over all frequencies with a weighting function

Period: A measure of wave repeatability. The wave period is considered as the time between two successive crests.

Peak period (Tp): The period with the maximum wave energy, determined from the wave spectrum.

Refraction: The process by which the direction of a moving wave is changed due to its interaction with the bottom topography. Wave heights may be increased or decreased by refraction.

Rip current: A strong surface current of short duration flowing seaward from the shore. It usually appears as a visible band of agitated water and is the return movement of water piled up on the shore by incoming waves and wind. Often referred to as a rip tide.

Rule of thumb: The act of hold out your hand, sticking your thumb in the air, and gauging the Kentucky Windage to gain a decent estimate for most cases. See Kentucky Windage.

Set: A group of waves. See Wave Group.

Shoaling: Changes in wave height as waves move into shallow water. Except for a limited depth region, shoaling increases wave heights. Shoaling occurs even if wave heights and directions do not change as a result of wave refraction.

Significant Wave Height (Hs): This is the average of the highest 1/3 of all waves in a time series.

Significant Wave Period (Ts): The average period of the one-third highest waves in a wave record.

Soup: That white foamy brew left over from a crashing wave. Not intended for human consumption, although it tends to consume humans.

Spectrum: A method of representing the distribution of wave energy as a function of frequency.

SST: Sea surface temperature.

Standout Spot: A break that has bigger waves in comparison to nearby surf spots as a result of shoaling and refraction.

Steepness: Ratio of wave height to wavelength.

Stoke: That awesome feeling you get when you ride a wave. Stoke is the fuel that powers the soul of the water sport enthusiast.

Trough: The lowest part of the wave between successive crests.

UTC (Universal Time Coordinate): Same as GMT. This is the time at the zero degree meridian crossing through Greenwich, England.

Wave Decay: The change which occurs in waves when they leave a fetch and pass through a region of lighter winds.

Wave Dispersion: see Dispersion.

Wave Group: A series of waves propagating together in which the wave direction, wavelength, and wave height vary only slightly. Wave groups that approach the shore are known as "sets".

Wavelength: The distance between the crest of one wave to the crest of the next wave.

Wave Spectrum: The distribution of wave energy among different wave frequencies of wavelengths on the sea surface.

Wave Train: A series of waves from the same direction, e.g. a swell.

APPENDIX A

Conversions

This section contains some common conversions used throughout this book, in our WaveCast® reports, and data on the Internet used for surf and weather forecasting.

Celsius to Fahrenheit

°C	°F	°C	°F	°C	°F	°C	°F
50	122.0	27	80.6	4	39.2	-19	-2.2
49	120.2	26	78.8	3	37.4	-20	-4.0
48	118.4	25	77.0	2	35.6	-21	-5.8
47	116.6	24	75.2	1	33.8	-22	-7.6
46	114.8	23	73.4	0	32.0	-23	-9.4
45	113.0	22	71.6	-1	30.2	-24	-11.2
44	111.2	21	69.8	-2	28.4	-25	-13.0
43	109.4	20	68.0	-3	26.6	-26	-14.8
42	107.6	19	66.2	-4	24.8	-27	-16.6
41	105.8	18	64.4	-5	23.0	-28	-18.4
40	104.0	17	62.6	-6	21.2	-29	-20.2
39	102.2	16	60.8	-7	19.4	-30	-22.0
38	100.4	15	59.0	-8	17.6	-31	-23.8
37	98.6	14	57.2	-9	15.8	-32	-25.6

°C	°F	°C	°F	°C	°F	°C	°F
36	96.8	13	55.4	-10	14.0	-33	-27.4
35	95.0	12	53.6	-11	12.2	-34	-29.2
34	93.2	11	51.8	-12	10.4	-35	-31.0
33	91.4	10	50.0	-13	8.6	-36	-32.8
32	89.6	9	48.2	-14	6.8	-37	-34.6
31	87.8	8	46.4	-15	5.0	-38	-36.4
30	86.0	7	44.6	-16	3.2	-39	-38.2
29	84.2	6	42.8	-17	1.4	-40	-40.0
28	82.4	5	41.0	-18	-0.4		

Knots and MPH

1 knot = 1.15 mph
1 mph = 0.87 knot

Meters and Feet

1 meters = 3.28 feet
1 foot = 0.30 meters

Nautical Miles and Miles

1 nautical mile = 1.15 miles
1 mile = 0.87 nautical miles

Kilometers and Miles

1 kilometer = 0.62 miles
1 mile = 1.61 kilometers

APPENDIX B

Wind to Wave Scale

This section contains tables showing wind speeds from isobar spacing as well as our modified versions of the famous Beaufort scale to calculate wave heights and period based on wind speed. These tables are useful if you do not have access to the Internet and cannot access the WAM's, yet you have access to pressure maps or other means to forecast wind and fetch.

It's important to note that the height of waves in a fetch is controlled by three primary factors:

- Wind speed
- Wind duration
- Fetch (the distance over water that the wind blows in a single direction).

Any one of these factors may limit the wave height. If the wind speed is low, large waves are not produced, no matter how long the wind blows over an unlimited fetch. If the wind speed is great, but it blows for only a few minutes, no high waves are produced despite unlimited wind strength and fetch.

The four tables included in this appendix are:

1. **Table B-1**: Wind speeds derived from isobar spacing. This is from 4mb readings (sea level). If you are using 300mb pressure maps, you may want to subtract 30–40% from the wind speeds to estimate 4mb readings.

2. **Table B-2 Minimum duration fetch**: This shows how long it would take wind to blow over a fetch to create a certain wave height and period. This is ideal for large ground swell storms, and some wind swell

systems. This however is not ideal for hurricanes that travel quickly, and do not create a vast area of fetch.

3. **Table B-3 Typical Hurricane Durations**: Since hurricanes travel quickly, and tend to have smaller areas of fetch, these times are more realistic for forecasting swell from tropical cyclones.

4. **Table B-4 24–48 Hour Durations:** This table is similar to B-2, but shows some durations of only 24 and 48 hours.

Table B-1: Wind Speeds from Isobar Spacing

Note: The spacing of isobars is inversely proportional to the wind speed. In other words, the greater the wind speed, the smaller the spacing. For a given wind speed, the spacing between isobars decreases with increasing latitude; thus, the following table shows wind speeds based on 4 different latitudes: 30°, 40°, 50°, and 60°.

This table refers to sea level reading (4mb). For 300mb or 500mb readings, you may want to subtract an additional 30–40% from the wind speeds to estimate the 4mb sea level readings.

Wind speed (kt)	Approximate distance (in nautical miles) between isobars			
	30°	40°	50°	60°
10	461	358	301	266
15	307	239	200	177
20	230	179	150	133
25	184	143	120	106
30	154	119	100	89
35	132	102	86	76
40	115	90	75	66
50	92	72	60	53
60	77	60	50	44

Figure 43 Table B-1 Isobar Spacing Wind Speeds (4mb)

The terms in the following tables are:

- **Wind**: wind speed in knots.
- **Duration**: minimum length of time in hours that wind continues to blow at this speed.
- **Height**: wave heights in feet resulting from this fetch.
- **Period**: period in seconds contained in this fetch.

Table B-2: Minimum Duration for Fetch

Wind	Duration	Height	Period
0	0	0	0
1–3	0.25	0.25	1
4–6	0.5	0.5	2
7–10	2	1	3
11–16	5	3	4
17–21	10	5	6
22–27	15	13	10
28–33	24	22	12
34–40	36	37	14
41–47	48	57	17
48–55	72	80	19
56–63	96	100	23
64–71+	108	120	24

Table B-3: Typical Hurricane Durations

Wind	Duration	Height	Period
60	4	18	10
60	8	25	11
60	12	30	12
70	4	22	11
70	8	34	12
70 .	12	40	13
80	4	30	12
80	8	40	13
80	12	50	14
90	4	35	12
90	8	50	14
90	12	60	15
100	4	38	13
100	8	55	15
100	12	70	16
110	4	42	14
110	8	65	16
110	12	80	18
120	4	50	14
120	8	70	17
120	12	90	21

Table B-4: 24–48 Hour Durations

Wind	Duration	Height	Period
10	24	2	4
10	48	3	5
20	24	8	6
20	48	10	8
30	24	19	9
30	48	22	10
40	24	25	11
40	48	30	12
50	24	35	13
50	48	45	14
60	24	55	16
60	48	65	19
70+	24	65	19
70+	48	80	22

Acknowledgements
and References

This book is the product of our brief knowledge on the science of oceanography, and based mainly on years of experience. As such, some other people took the time to answer some questions, and many resources were used for research to provide as much accuracy as possible.

Many thanks to Dr. Robert Stewart from the Oceanography Department at Texas A&M University for all his patience and informative answers. Thank you Dr. Stewart for taking the time, and providing information in an easy to understand manner, in your correspondence, and a fantastically informative web site at http://oceanworld.tamu.edu/

I'd like to extend a special thanks to Ernest Knowles, PhD—Alumni Distinguished Undergraduate Professor Oceanography Department of Marine, Earth & Atmospheric Sciences at NCSU, for his information on seasonal currents, and taking time out of his busy schedule to guide us in the right direction.

Many concepts in basic wave theory were researched for accuracy using:

- *Introduction to Physical Oceanography*, by Dr. Robert H. Stewart, which can be found on the web at: http://oceanworld.tamu.edu/resources/ocng_textbook/contents.html

- *NSW Coastline Management Manual*, located on the web at: http://ea.gov.au/coasts/publications/nswmanual/index.html

Wave measurement techniques were partially researched from *Introduction to the World's Oceans* by Alyn C. Dusbury

Various calculations were researched from:

- *Ocean Surface Waves, Their Physics and Prediction*, by Stanislaw R. Massel, Australian Institute of Marine Science

- *The Aerographer's Advanced Training Series* at http://www.tpub.com/weather3/

Portions of the rip current hazard were excerpt from *NOAA News* at http://www.noaanews.noaa.gov/magazine/stories/mag48.htm

Information on flags and postings was researched at the United States Lifesaving Association web site at http://www.usla.org.

Some weather information on storm formation was researched and excerpt from: http://www.usatoday.com/weather/resources/basics/wworks0.htm

Information on the PDO was researched and excerpt from: http://tao.atmos.washington.edu/pdo/

Beaufort scale calculations were partially derived from the *Global Guide to Tropical Cyclone Forecasting* by the Bureau of Meteorology Research Centre, Melbourne, Victoria, Australia, which can be found on the web at http://www.bom.gov.au/bmrc/pubs/tcguide/globa_guide_intro.htm.

Isobar spacing wind speed table was expert from the *Aerographer's Intermediate Training Series* on the web at http://www.tpub.com/weather2/.

Storm tracking maps, wave analysis models, and buoy data images, are provided from the National Weather Service, CDIP, NCEP, and NOAA. Additionally, Figure 8 was provide by La Jolla surfing. These are available from public domain, and per Title 17 U.S.C. 403, are not part of the copyrighted material in this book.

Global view of the Earth in Chapter 2 is provided by NationalAtlas.gov. This is available from public domain, and per Title 17 U.S.C. 403, is not part of the copyrighted material in this book. "National Atlas of the United States®" and "The National Atlas of the United States of America®" are registered trademarks of the United States Department of the Interior.

0-595-30365-X

Printed in the United States
21356LVS00005B/133

9 780595 303656